MEMOIRS *of*
a SOLDIER
in the
HOUSEHOLD
CAVALRY

GW00645478

Walkmill Publishing

© Jack Shortman 2003
Memoirs of a Soldier in the Household Cavalry

Second edition with revisions 2010

ISBN 978-0-9543090-0-8

Published by:
Walkmill Publishing
12 Wilfred Owen Avenue
Oswestry
Shropshire
SY11 2NB

Design & production co-ordinated by:
The *Better Book* Company Ltd
5 Lime Close
Chichester
West Sussex
PO19 6SW

Printed in England

CONTENTS

FOREWORD

I read Mr. Shortman's memoirs of his service in the Household Cavalry with great interest since his years of service coincided with a period when I was actively engaged in various roles within the Household Cavalry. The picture he paints is a light hearted one very true to life as it was in the Regiment in those days. He joined at Hadrian's Camp, Carlisle in 1955 and it had been my duty in 1951 to launch the Household Cavalry element in the 67th RAC Training Regiment at Carlisle. The Royal Armoured Corps at that time were not very well disposed towards the Household Cavalry whom they regarded, presumably because of our ceremonial role, as over privileged and having customs, which did not conform to those of the Royal Armoured Corps. I confess that I did not find it too easy to start with but fairly quickly we adjusted to our different habits and eventually all went well.

Mr. Shortman's picture of life in the Regiment is very true to form and I commend and congratulate him on producing such a humorous record of what must have been a very important phase in his life.

THE DUKE OF WELLINGTON KG

ACKNOWLEDGEMENTS

I never really meant to write this chronicle, but my wife Mary and my family persuaded me that at the very least I should put down the account of my army life on paper.

What I have written is true to the best of my knowledge and my memory. I have tried to write down the events as I saw them and I hope I have not offended anyone in the process and that I have not got any of these events or procedures wrong.

I would like to thank Roy Cook, Malcolm Barker, Charlie Harrison, Barry Lewis, George Dugdale and Pete Hitchcock for their memories and their help.

Lastly I would like to thank my old friend Doug Skelly, as without Doug's understanding and friendship I would not have finished this chronicle. Sadly Doug passed away before he could read this, so Doug old friend this is dedicated to you, sleep well old friend.

I would like to express my special thanks to Clifford Cooke, because without his bravery and trust this book would not have been published.

JS

INTRODUCTION

The Lifeguards and the Blues and Royals were formed in 1660 and 1661 to provide mounted escorts for the Monarch.

Several thousand men have passed through the ranks of both Regiments and this is the story of just one.

The author began his army career as a National Service man in 1955 with the Royal Horse Guards serving at Carlisle, Windsor and Cyprus.

After his demob in 1957 and not liking the civilian life he re-enlisted in 1960 in the same Regiment. He served with the Mounted Regiment then went back to the Mechanised Regiment in Windsor and Germany.

In 1969 the Regiment was amalgamated with the Royals. Because he was unable to transfer, the author was demobbed and re-enlisted into the Royal Artillery and thence to the Life Guards where he finished his service.

The author has enlivened his text with strong human anecdotes and has gathered together many photographs of people and places that enhance the story.

MEMOIRS OF A SOLDIER IN THE HOUSEHOLD CAVALRY

Part One

CHAPTER ONE

CARLISLE

I first joined the Armed Services on 23 June 1955 as a National Serviceman at the tender age of eighteen after completing three years as an apprentice bricklayer. I could have stayed on until I was twenty, but I decided that I wanted to get this part of my life over and done with.

I received my call-up papers and was told to report to Hadrian's Camp near Carlisle. As I had never travelled further than Oswestry it was with some trepidation that I caught the train from Shrewsbury on a bright and sunny morning.

The journey seemed endless, broken only by other young lads joining the train at various points, all like me destined for Carlisle. We eventually arrived at the station and we were met by a very tall man in Army uniform with sergeant stripes on his sleeve. This turned out to be our Squad Instructor and his rank was Corporal of the Horse and his Regiment was the Life Guards.

We all piled onto Army trucks and we were whisked away to our new 'home'. The Camp was situated some three miles outside the town and when we arrived and disembarked we were sorted out into 'Squads' of some 25 men per Squad. We were shown where we would be sleeping and where to 'draw up' our bedding and on completion of this task we were once again 'fell in' in Squads and marched to the Quartermaster's Stores where we were to 'draw up' our kit.

This kit consisted of everything that we would need from a uniform to underclothes and the necessary webbing for a lance corporal called FSMO which translated was Full Service Marching Order. This webbing consisted of what seemed like 101 different bits of webbing with bits of tarnished brass fitments of various shapes and sizes.

Hadrian's Camp Carlisle, intake 55/12 Squad Four, June/July 1955

Top rank TPRS Baker (LG) Stephenson (RHG) Jeeves (RHG)

Rear TPRS Ellis (RHG) Scotchbrook (RHG) Cook (RHG) Hunt (RHG) Pashley (RHG), Peters, Prior

Centre TPRS Williams (726 RHG) Williams (402 RHG) Murphy (RAC) Callan (RAC) Bolo (RAC) Ragley (RAC) Scarlett (RHG) Shortman (RHG)

Front TPRS Keeling (RAC) Seventy (RAC) Pigg (RAC) COH Wakefield (LG) Hopkins (RAC) Hockings (RAC) Killin (RAC)

It was quite funny really when we were being issued with this kit. We all stood in line and when it was my turn I was asked what hat size I took, and not having had the pleasure of ever wearing a hat of any description I replied that I did not know. The reply was instantaneous, "Six and Seven Eights," screamed the storeman and slapped a beret into my hands and yelled "next". I was shunted to the next part of the long counter where another storeman was waiting with a tape measure.

"Raise your arms to shoulder height and then bend your elbows, pointing your hands to the front," he hissed at me. Doing what I was told he commenced to measure my dimensions. After a very quick, "chest 38, neck 14, waist 28, inside leg 32," yet another storeman piled two pairs of trousers, two tunics and three shirts into my arms.

I was shunted on once more to another storeman (they all looked alike to me) and about to contemplate that there was only one storeman really and he was dashing up and down handing out this kit, when I was somewhat startled by a voice shouting in an aggrieved way asking if I was, "Bloody well deaf and what size boots did I bloody well take?"

I shouted back that I took a size ten and was quickly told in no uncertain fashion that I did not speak that way to a 'trained soldier' and that next time I would be on a 'fizzer' for sure. Having no idea what constituted a 'fizzer' I wrongly assumed that this was some sort of ritual which all new recruits had to endure and I ignored the 'trained soldier' in question. I was to find out the hard way what was meant by being on a 'fizzer' to my cost.

The issuing of kit went on for some time with the handing out of underwear, socks, buttons, boot brushes and cleaning kit. The last item given to me was a cap badge, which turned out to be the Royal Armoured Corps badge. The design was a cluster of leaves enclosing a mailed fist. The Corps was made up of various Cavalry Regiments which were either equipped with tanks or armoured cars, but more of this later.

When we had been issued with all our kit and taken it back to our assigned barrack block we were shown by our 'trained soldier' how to make our beds the Army way. We were told where to find the cookhouse to get our evening meal. We all seemed famished and set off looking forward to a good meal. We were vastly disappointed as the meal consisted of mashed potatoes, beans and what we took to be a pork chop. Most of us left it.

We were told that we could not go to the NAAFI (Navy, Army and Air Force Institute) that evening as we had to get all our kit sorted out and that lights out would be at 10.30 p.m. So that was the end of my first day in the Army.

We were all aroused the following morning at 5.30 a.m. This consisted in the first instance with the sound of a bugle, which none of us took the slightest bit of notice of. In the second instance we were rudely awakened by the terrific noise of a stick being banged against a dustbin lid, which was wielded by a trained soldier, together with the cry, "Everyone out of bed, dressed and fall in outside for roll call."

Those that desisted even this noise were rudely tipped out of their beds by the trained soldier, who we thought had really gone berserk. We all managed to dress somehow in strange attire and stagger outside where we were met by a very smartly dressed lance corporal. When I say smartly dressed I mean he was immaculate from his gleaming boots to his spotless beret. At what time this man had risen to dress himself like that my imagination boggled.

After we had all answered our names we were told that breakfast was in fifteen minutes and that we had to be back in the barrack room by 6.30 a.m., where we would be shown how to lay out our kit. We all trooped off to the cookhouse with some trepidation remembering last night's evening meal. This time we were not disappointed. Breakfast consisted of beans once again, (probably left over from our meal last night) a piece of charred bacon and a fried egg that was extremely hard.

Upon returning to the barrack room we were all grouped around one bed where we were shown how to 'box' our blankets, sheets and pillowcases. We had been issued with a green blanket with a black line running down the centre. This we had to cover the mattress with, ensuring that the black line ran straight down the middle of the said mattress.

We were then shown a diagram of how and where to lay out all our kit. This had to be done each morning before first parade, which it seemed was 7.45 a.m. I quietly pointed out to the immaculate Lance Corporal the fact that this would take approximately thirty minutes and that as we rose at 5.30 a.m. by the time we had washed, shaved, had roll call, gone to breakfast and returned that there would not be enough time to do a half decent job of laying out our kit.

This observation proved to be my first mistake of my Army career. It seemed that one did not make those kind of observations to immaculately dressed Lance Corporals, even if it seemed a logical observation. Logic, I soon came to understand, was not a thing Lance Corporals were endowed with, in fact they probably didn't know what the word meant.

If this particular Lance Corporal had been a hot air balloon he would have probably broken all records for the highest ascent, "Won't have time, won't have time," he spluttered. "Then you will have to make time, won't you, you horrible man. Get up earlier or miss breakfast, but this kit *will* be laid out by 07.45 hours, is that understood?" We all nodded furiously. He glared at me, "This time I'll let this pass, but next time you'll be on a 'fizzer' so fast your feet won't touch, right."

"Right," I replied. My second 'clanger'.

He went into orbit again, "Right what?" he exploded.

"Er, right Sir," I guessed. Third clanger.

"Right Lance Corporal, is what you say," he fumed. "You don't call me Sir, understand."

"I understand, Lance Corporal," I replied.

"That's better, don't you forget."

This scintillating conversation was broken up by the sound of another bugle call. "All right you lot everyone outside and fall in." This it seemed was 'First Parade'. We all assembled outside and were ordered to "Fall in" in three ranks (there were twenty four in my Squad). We all managed to get in some sort of order and the

Lance Corporal called out our names. We were then ordered to come to attention. The Lance Corporal marched off to report us present and correct.

After a wait of about fifteen minutes a voice somewhere in the distance shouted an order, whereupon another immaculate soldier marched over to our Squad. He halted in front of us and in a voice that was probably heard in the town centre ordered us to stand at ease. This was our Squad Instructor and he introduced himself as Corporal of the Horse Wakefield and that his Regiment was The Life Guards.

The days seemed to merge into one long, what seemed to me, chaotic life style from reveille to lights out. Cleaning kit, laying out kit, foot drill, rifle drill, never ending. This routine was only broken twice in the five weeks of 'Square Bashing' before our 'Passing out Parade'.

The first was a trip to the local Army Firing Ranges where we were to fire our Lee Enfield 303 rifles for the first time. The emphasis on this range was safety first and a certain drill was to be adhered to at all times. It was with a thrill and with some trepidation that I stepped forward onto the firing range.

I had been thoroughly tested in the routine on the firing point on a number of occasions on a mock firing point in barracks. Everything went smoothly and I even managed to put some rounds into the target, much to my and the instructor's surprise. We did several trips to that range over the next few weeks and this training was to stand me in good stead later on in my career.

The second deviation from the day-to-day routine happened one day after the Squad's first period of drill. Little but did I know that this day would be the day that I commenced my Army career as a Household Cavalryman. We were ordered to fall in and were marched down to the Quartermaster's Stores where we were to be issued with our individual Regimental shoulder flashes and cap badges.

I was, probably because I was quite tall, issued with a shoulder flash, blue with the words Royal Horse Guards embroidered in red and a cap badge, brown in colour (I was later to be told that it was

67th Training Regt. Wireless Wing Hadrians Camp Carlisle Aug-Oct 1955
Troopers Ellis Shortman Scotchbrook Murphy Bagley Peterson Brown Stone Davidson Biggs Hampson (LCPL Adams CPL Bellamy instructors)
Trooper Clark Louch

made of a bakelite material) again with the name of the Regiment around the rim. I was then informed that I was now a Guardsman. I was also issued with a new type of headgear, a forage cap. This was made of some cardboard type material covered in khaki cloth. Two small brass buttons were to be sewn onto each side of this cap so that a leather chinstrap could be attached.

Two or three mornings per week we had PT as our first parade. Our dress consisted of socks, plimsolls, shorts that seemed ten sizes too big and a red or white PT vest. PT consisted of, in those days, simply jumping up and down and moving our arms around culminating in running around the gym a few times.

But on one occasion we arrived in the gym to find a boxing ring had been erected. We were paired off and told we would have to box for one minute. I was paired with Trooper Bagley and while watching the others perform we hit upon a plan so that neither of us got hurt. I for one had no intention of getting belted in the face for no apparent reason.

Our plan was simple, when we got into the ring we would pretend to spar around for the minute and that would be that. However, well laid plans often go astray, as did this plan. The moment we touched gloves in the middle of the ring, Trooper Bagley hit me on the nose causing it to bleed. Not liking this one bit I hit him back as hard as I could.

We went at it then for the whole of the prescribed time having to be separated at the end. When I asked Bagley later why he did not stick to the plan he said he did not know why, it just seemed the right thing to do in case I hit him first. I think I learned a lesson from that.

The daily routine continued and the Squad was now getting its act together. We were better at drill, better at cleaning kit and laying out kit and there was a comradeship forming, a comradeship that was to last until my demob. Finally at last the great day arrived, our 'Passing Out Parade'.

We were all in a state of great excitement on that Friday in July. Not only were we all 'Passing Out' and going to our different Regiments, some like me were returning to Carlisle for trade training, but we were also going on an extended weekend leave. The Parade went like clockwork and afterwards we all had a drink in the NAAFI and presented CoH Wakefield with a leather wallet when for once the old soldier was lost for words. I came across Harry Wakefield again many years later, but that's another chapter in my life.

The goodbyes were said as we all collected our travel warrants. Those who were returning and those who were in my Regiment I would meet again, but the others, whom I had shared laughter and yes tears with, I was never to see again at least up and to this day.

I cannot recollect much about the weekend leave, suffice to say that it was a never ending round of relations who wanted to see me in my smart uniform. I remember that I was secretly glad when my leave was up and I caught the train back to Carlisle.

Our accommodation was now in another part of the camp and the routine was now rather more relaxed, no more laying out our kit every day, it was now once a week on a Friday morning. Now provided your particular room was good enough you were each allowed a local pass to go into the town over the weekend, provided you were not on Guard duty.

I recall my first trip down town. I had made friends with a chap from Birmingham, Wally Pitt, and we had decided to make a night of it in the town dance hall, together with the usual round of pubs. We both painstakingly cleaned our kit as we all had to be in uniform to go down town and paraded ourselves for inspection at the Guard room. After a minute inspection we were let out of the main gate. There was a handy bus stop across the road and in due course one came along and we duly arrived in the town centre.

We had all been warned of the 'wages of sin and drink' so we headed for what looked like a respectable bar. Now the wages of a National Serviceman were very low and I think I received after sending some money home, about ten shillings per week. After buying the necessary cleaning items there was very little left over. However my friend and I had contrived to 'Buy' a night guard or two, which paid a pound a go, a lot of money in those days. Therefore on this particular night we had combined our wealth and were well placed financially.

After a few pints of the local ale, I had not drunk much before this time, we arrived outside the local dance hall and managed with some difficulty to obtain a ticket, which we had to show if we wanted a pass out for alcoholic refreshments as none were served on the premises.

To cut a long story short we managed to latch onto two young ladies who were in Carlisle on holiday with relations. We managed to persuade them that they needed an escort to their dwelling place and we duly took them home. Before parting we arranged to meet them in Birmingham for a weekend, we had a weekend pass due half way through our course and both of us caught the bus back to camp rather jubilant at the evening being such a success.

I now settled down to my training as a Radio Operator. This, to me, was a very interesting course and I soon entered into the course with great enthusiasm. I will always be grateful to the Instructors for teaching me well as this trade was to lead to promotion later on in my career. We slogged on learning voice procedure, the phonetic alphabet, that is exchanging words for each letter, e.g. the letter A becomes ALPHA and so on.

We also had to learn how to open a Radio Net of several stations and communicate between all of them. Various 'Exercises' were planned for this course, including outside the camp area. At the end of each week we were tested on what we had been taught.

By the fourth week we were all getting quite proficient at opening and closing radio sets and sending messages, but what was really on our minds was leave. We were all due a 48 hour pass. This time was calculated from after duties on the Friday until 2359 hours on the Sunday. The term 48 hours was erroneous really because by the time you had caught your train, the train journey in those days from Carlisle to where I lived was some four or five hours, the Friday evening was a washout. Also by the time you had visited all family and friends it was time to catch the train back.

However any time spent away from the Army regime was time well spent, or so we thought. *The* Friday dawned and we could not wait to read daily orders, get our leave passes and get out of the barracks. My friend Wally and I had planned to meet the two young ladies in Birmingham, we had both written to them and received replies. We had both saved up some money and were set for a very pleasant weekend, that is, until we read daily orders.

Let me explain, daily orders were pinned up each day, usually in the evening, setting out the routine for the following day i.e. the soldiers who were on guard, fatigues and other duties. Brummie and I discovered, to our complete horror, that we had both been placed on cookhouse fatigues on the Saturday morning which meant that we could not get away until long after lunch time. This meant that we would not be able to arrive in Birmingham until late Saturday night and we would have to start our return journey at about lunch time on the Sunday, therefore completely ruining the weekend.

We could not let the young ladies know of this change in time, phones were only for the very well off in those days. Brummie and I both dashed around trying to 'sell' the fatigues but as you may realise no one wanted to know. What could we do, we were determined to have our weekend. We decided to go and to hell with it, have a good weekend and face the consequences when we returned.

We had tea and thought up a plan. If we booked out at the Guard room we would be absent from 2359 hours, so we decided to jump over the fence surrounding the camp and make our way to the railway station, we managed to have enough money for our fares as we could not get rail warrants. This we managed to do, duly caught a train and arrived in Birmingham. Suffice to say that we both had a marvellous weekend. On the train back we decided that we had to jump the fence back and hope we had not been missed, although this was only a faint hope, we knew we were in serious trouble. We duly arrived in Carlisle and managed to catch the last bus back to camp. We found a suitable spot in the fence the furthest away from the main gate and climbed over. With our hearts in our mouths we made our way to our barrack room, undressed climbed into bed and waited for the outburst in the morning.

We woke and went to breakfast, our last in freedom we thought.

Talking with the other soldiers in our room they had all had a good weekend, but knew nothing of our absence. It was with some trepidation that Wally and I fell in on first parade that morning. Our names were called and we duly fell out and went along to our course classrooms but nothing was said. During all that day we were both on tenterhooks but nothing was said or done. What had happened?

We talked it over and came to the conclusion that the Orderly Corporal for that Saturday had not taken our names down for fatigues and that fearing the consequences had not bothered to report the fact that we were absent. We never did find out what really happened. I still see Wally from time to time and we always discuss this episode in our lives. We both came to the conclusion that we both learned a lesson which would stand us in good stead later on in our Army careers.

The remaining four weeks seemed to fly and it dawned the day of our course examinations. I seemed to have taken to this particular trade very well and duly passed the exam with flying colours, so did Wally. All that remained now were leave passes and travel warrants to our various Regiments. There were three of us on this course, Wally and I and a chap whose name I cannot remember. He was a regular soldier and he was demobbed not long before the Regiment departed for overseas duties.

We all bid farewell to Hadrian's Camp and to our Instructors and to the many friends we had made who were going off to their own Regiments. Wally and I made arrangements to see each other during our leave, together with the young ladies from Birmingham who we still wrote to. We parted at Crewe station and this was the start of another adventure.

CHAPTER TWO

THE REGIMENT

After the chaotic events over the last thirteen weeks I became bored with inactivity after one week's leave. It was therefore with some relief and great excitement that I boarded a train for London. Apparently I had to change at Paddington for a train to Windsor. This was no mean feat for anyone who had to carry as much kit as I had to.

It was a cold and wet day in October, but I sweated with all this kit. I eventually arrived at Paddington station and was directed to another platform where I had to wait about an hour for the next train. I remember sitting down on a bench to wait, I had very little money to buy a cup of tea, when I was accosted by another soldier asking if this was the platform for the Windsor train. He was also Royal Horse Guards but a regular soldier who had done his training at a place called Pirbright, which I learned later was the Brigade of Guards' depot.

Our train eventually arrived and we piled on. I noticed several other soldiers along the platform among them the rest of my Squad from Carlisle. We all got together and swapped stories of our leave. We arrived at Windsor at about 7 a.m. we had to report by first parade and there was a three ton Army wagon waiting outside the station with a lance corporal in charge. We all answered our names and climbed aboard.

On the journey to the barracks we passed Windsor castle and caught a glimpse of the smart Guardsman outside the main gate. The barracks turned out to be the other side of the town, it had a name, Combermere Barracks. Little but did I know at this time that this barracks was to be my home on and off for a good number of years. There was another barracks in the town and that was Victoria Barracks which housed a Battalion of one of Her Majesty's Foot

Guards, who did the Royal duties at the castle.

We all jumped off the three tonner and were met by a CoH who led us over to the Regimental Orderly Room where we were to be 'processed' he said. This apparently meant that we would be allocated to different Squadrons. The Regiment was made up of what we would learn to be three Sabre Squadrons and a Headquarters Squadron, the Sabre Squadrons being the 'Fighting'Squadrons and HQ Squadron the administration Squadron.

I and my new found friend were told to report to A Squadron. I had looked for my mate Wally, but had not seen him. I discovered later that he had received fresh posting orders whilst on leave to report to Pirbright and it was quite a long time before I was to see him again. My new found friend, Pete Hitchcocks, and I reported to A Squadron office where we were met by the Squadron Corporal Major, SCM 'Slash' Peake.

The reason he was affectionately called this is because when we were issued our forage caps the peaks stuck out like a helicopter landing pad, so we used to cut away the stitches and push up the peak so that it lay almost flat on one's forehead but this particular SCM did not do this, hence the nickname.

This may seem a funny rank, let me explain. In the two Regiments of the Household Cavalry, that is The Royal Horse Guards and the Life Guards both have a completely different rank structure than any other Regiment in the British Army. The whys and the wherefores are too complicated to set down in this journal so I will keep it simple.

The first rank in the Regiment is a Lance Corporal who wears two stripes on his upper sleeve with a brass crown over them. The next rank is a full Corporal, who in those days wore the same two stripes and a crown. The modern rank is three stripes and a cloth crown.

The next rank is three stripes and a brass crown which is called a Corporal of the Horse, abbreviated to CoH. Next comes a rank called a Squadron Quartermaster Corporal or a SQMC, which is equivalent to a Staff Sergeant. Next comes a Squadron Corporal

Major, a SCM or WO2. The highest rank within the Regiment is the Regimental Corporal Major, RCM or WO1.

There are three other ranks of importance within the Regiment. The Orderly Room Quartermaster Corporal, he is the Chief Clerk of the Regiment, the Technical Quartermaster Corporal, he is the senior rank in the Technical Stores, and lastly, the Regimental Quartermaster Corporal, the senior rank in the Quartermaster's Stores.

The SCM of A Squadron informed us which troop we would be placed in. Pete and I would be in 4 Troop. The Squadron Orderly Corporal told us where the Squadron barrack block was and we humped our kit over to a three storey building. This building dated back many years and there were horse stables underneath. We were housed on the middle floor. The barrack room was much different from the barrack rooms of Hadrian's Camp.

They housed about twenty soldiers and the furniture was sparse to say the least. Each of us had a locker, these were all in the middle of the room, and each of us had a wall locker above our bed. We unpacked our kit and deposited it in the lockers. There was one soldier in the room who turned out to be a sort of room orderly.

Each resident of the room took it in turns to look after the room so that no lockers could be broken open and to keep the coal fire replenished as this was the only means of heating this very large room. I was to find out the hard way how the coal bunker in the room was kept topped up.

We found out from him where the bedding stores were and more importantly where the NAAFI was. Pete and I then drew up our bedding and dumped it in the room and shot off to have a NAAFI break. After this we returned to the barrack room and made up our beds copying the beds next to us.

We discovered from the room orderly that we only laid out our kit when ordered to do so by the troop officer, which was roughly once a month. This was to check your kit to see if there was anything missing. What a joy this was, not having to lay out all your kit even once a week.

We were also told by the room orderly that the Squadron had a parade at two o'clock and as we had been told to do nothing else we were left to ourselves. Lunch time came and we found our way to the cookhouse and had what we thought was an excellent meal, by Carlisle standards anyway.

We noticed that during the meal that an officer and a CoH came around the dining area. Apparently this was the Orderly Officer and the Orderly CoH. They would stop at some table and ask if the meal was OK. Normally the answer would be, "Yes, Sir." Any other answer might bring down the wrath of the Master Cook.

Pete and I wandered outside at about 1350 hours and joined the rest of the Squadron soldiers as they waited for the 1400 hours parade. A lance corporal told us where to fall in with the other members of 4 Troop. The names were called out by the Squadron Orderly Corporal, who then reported to the SCM that the Squadron was present.

The SCM would normally report to an officer, but as there were no officers present he ordered that the Troop NCOs (Non Commissioned Officers) carry on. They in turn ordered us to fall out. We were told by the Troop Lance Cororal to go around to the troop lines where the Troop armoured cars were parked.

I had been posted at the wrong time as it was the build up to the Regiment's annual Admin Inspection before handing over to the Life Guards, who were returning from the Middle East to take over my Regiment's duties in UK whilst we went over to the Middle East. Therefore the armoured vehicles had to be cleaned and maintained to a very high standard.

I was detailed to be a Radio Operator in a Daimler armoured car and Pete was to be the other Daimler's gunner. The troop consisted of two Daimlers and two Dingos. The Dingos were a sort of armoured car without a turret. The Daimler's crew consisted of a Commander, Driver, Gunner and Radio Operator, the Dingo's crew, Commander and Driver.

The rest of the day passed with getting to know the insides of my AFV and getting to know the crew, who seemed to be decent enough fellows, some were National Servicemen like myself and others were regular soldiers, some with a number of years' service.

We packed in work at about 1630 hours and returned to our troop room to clean up before tea. Pete and I went to read Squadron Orders. We were not on guard, so I accosted the Squadron Orderly Corporal and asked if we were allowed down town if we were free of duty.

He informed us that we were allowed, but we must be in uniform, best uniform, best boots and belt. He warned us that if we were found to be in s... we would not be allowed out and also we would be on a 'fizzer'. "Don't try to go out before the night guard mounts," he advised. The Provost CoH, a certain CoH who was of somewhat dubious Scottish origin, would have your 'Guts for garters' if he inspected you and found the slightest thing wrong. We decided to take this advice.

Pete and I decided to go out that night about 8 o'clock, so we duly cleaned our kit (you were only allowed out in civilian clothes after you had completed six months' service and been issued with a permanent pass) and reported to the Guard room to 'Book out'. We had to march into the Guard room individually and halt at a white painted line about two feet from a desk and state your name, number, rank and ask permission to book out.

The Guard Commander then inspected you and if you were well 'Turned out' you were allowed out, but if you were not you were told to go and clean up whatever had been found at fault. This meant that you went back to your room, re-cleaned the offending item and then returned to the Guard room.

If the offending item was cleaned to the satisfaction of the Guard Commander you were allowed out, if not, back to the room or you were told you would not be let out anyway or you were on a 'fizzer' which would be dealt with the following day.

As our kit was in somewhat good condition from training, Pete and I were let out on our first night. We set off down into the town with high hopes of having a good night out. These hopes were soon to be dashed. We should have asked for information concerning the town and its pubs before embarking on the town.

The first pub proved to be a decent pub well patronised by our Regiment, but lacking excitement. We very quickly drank up and left. The second pub we entered we never got as far as the bar, we were forcefully evicted by a bunch of foot guards led by a huge man who informed us that this was a foot guards' pub and "Don't come back."

A little shaken we carried on up the main street and bumped into a member of the Regiment, also in uniform. He suggested that we try a pub near Windsor castle. We found this pub in a little cobbled street and entered. We ordered, found a table and sat down. Pete drew to my attention that there seemed to be a lack of female company in this particular pub, which seemed strange. There was also a lack of squaddies as far as we could tell.

It wasn't until a rather gaily dressed youth came to our table and asked us if we would like to go back to his place that it dawned on us that this pub was a meeting places for 'Gays'. As this subject was in those days taboo, we drank up and beat a very hasty retreat back to the original pub we had frequented. We both vowed to seek out our 'advisor' at the earliest opportunity and extract vengeance.

A couple of days later, this being a Saturday morning (in those days the Regiment worked on a Saturday until lunch time) Pete and I found ourselves on coal fatigues. The orders said that we were to report to the MT Office, MT meaning Military Transport, at 0815 hours. We duly reported and began the most dirty and hard working day I have ever spent. There were two men from each Squadron and when we had all arrived we climbed aboard a three ton truck and set off for the other barracks.

Upon arriving there we had to load up the truck with the Regiment's ration of coal. This meant shovelling coal into sacks and loading the sacks aboard the truck. The truck, we were informed by the Lance Corporal in charge, was only allowed to carry a limited amount of sacks in one trip and as we were loading several tons of coal it meant there would be several trips that day

The first trip saw us back at the barracks to unload. Each Squadron had detailed men to carry the sacks up to the barrack rooms, each room was allowed a number of sacks per week. We finished the last load late in the day and I was never more glad than to see the back of that truck. I never did another coal fatigue.

The days dragged on in general routine in cleaning up the vehicles and general maintenance. It was quite sometime before I found my name on orders for guard duty. This duty turned out to be on bonfire night. As this was my first guard I got the worst 'Stag'. You had to do two hours on and four hours off from 1800 hours until 0600 hours the following morning.

This meant that the worst two hours or 'Stag' were the second two hours. This was 2000 hours until 2200 hours, some left-over supper if you were lucky, and then 0200 hours until 0400 hours, which meant you didn't get much sleep. I was to find out that as you acquired more service you managed to get better 'Stags'.

At 2000 hours the sentries were marched around to their designated point of the barracks. I remember my post was the barrack field. Now in this barrack field were housed three Nissen huts, which were liberally painted with the signs DANGER AMMUNITION. My duty was to patrol around the outside of this barrack field.

By the time I had come on duty the bonfires and fireworks celebrations were in full swing and I began to notice with mounting alarm that an increasing number of sparks from the adjacent housing estate were beginning to fall around the three Nissen huts. This was not to mention the depleted rockets etc. that seemed to be descending all around.

I quickly ran to the field telephone that was connected to the Guard room and reported the fact that, in my estimation, there was going to be a rather large explosion very shortly and what was I supposed to do?

I was informed over the phone by a very angry Guard Commander, who had been dragged out of the Sergeants' Mess, not to be a silly ass and to get on with my sentry go. I spent the rest of my 'Stag' as far away from the barrack field as was possible. I discovered next day that the three Nissen huts only held discarded quartermaster equipment. It took some time to live down my first guard.

Came the day when we handed over all our vehicles and equipment to the advance party of the Life Guards. It also came on orders that all National Servicemen were to take the rest of their annual leave plus three weeks' embarkation leave. We were all jubilant, it meant that we would all have Christmas and the New Year at home.

But before this happened I blotted my copybook for the first time. I was busy one evening pressing my tunic, for I was on guard the next night, when the iron got too hot and I scorched the sleeve. We had been shown a trick by the old soldiers for this problem. The idea was to rub the offending area with a silver coin. I duly borrowed a silver sixpence and started to rub at the sleeve.

I must have rubbed too hard for, to my horror, a hole appeared in the cloth. I was in a state of panic for my other tunic was in the tailor's shop getting altered. My colleagues searched their lockers for a substitute tunic, but to no avail. Either they were too small, too big or the wrong tradesman flashes on the sleeves. There was no alternative, I had to repair the sleeve and hope it would be overlooked on the guard inspection.

I repaired it the best way I could, but it could not be hidden as it was on the front of the sleeve. Sure enough the Orderly Officer spotted the darn and I was duly charged. The following morning I was summoned to the Squadron office and amongst others awaited my turn to be marched in front of the Squadron Leader, Major Brayne-Nichols.

I was duly marched into his office and the charge read out by the Squadron Orderly Corporal. The Squadron Leader asked me what I had to say for myself and I told him what had happened. He sympathised with me, but found me guilty of damaging Army property and ordered me to forfeit one week's pay and that two shillings per week would be stopped from my pay until a new tunic was paid for.

This was a great blow to me, but not as much of a blow if he had given me seven days CB (confined to barracks). This punishment meant that not only would I have to parade every hour in different kit, but I would lose that much leave. I breathed a sigh of relief at the punishment. The SCM thought I had got away lightly and told me so in no uncertain terms.

The day dawned when we were to go on leave. I set out for the station with just a small pack with the necessary toilet things in, my civilian clothes were at home, and caught an early train arriving home around nine o'clock at night. I managed to get a couple of pints in before getting home.

I woke the next morning thinking, what will I do with myself for the next five weeks. Well I did find something to do, visiting friends and relations (again) and even managed to go down to Birmingham to meet up with my mate Wally again. The lucky so and so had wangled a posting to the tank depot at Bovington and had got his first stripe. Needless to say we had a wonderful time for the few days I stayed in Birmingham.

I also managed to travel to Leamington Spa where Pete lived. Pete and his family made me ever so welcome in their home and I will always remember that part of my leave with some amusement as Pete's family had a very odd sense of humour. Pete travelled up and spent a few days with me at my home and we managed to get some fishing in, which we both loved.

The last day of my leave proved almost to be a disaster. I had packed my things and left them at the station luggage office earlier in the day knowing that I would be slightly inebriated and that I might forget the bag.

It was only due to the intervention of my trusty uncle that I managed to catch the train at all. It was he who dragged me out of the pub, poured me into his car and managed to get me to the station in time. I was awoken at Paddington by a guard and pointed in the right direction for my train to Windsor. I fervently prayed that I would not be on guard that night.

Those returning from leave were in for a bit of a shock. Whereas before we were to take over from the Life Guards in Benghazi, Tripoli, the Life Guards' main party had been moved quickly to Cyprus to combat the upsurge of Greek/Turkish feeling about the island. An organisation called EOKA had been formed, which consisted of terrorists who thought that the island belonged to Greece.

We were all excited about this change in plans, but the

excitement was dulled by the thought that we would be on 'Active Service' footing during our stay out there, which would in fact be the rest of my National Service. The next few weeks were taken up by training in riot situations, both on foot and in our armoured cars. Each Squadron had to form another troop which was called Six Troop, which was formed as a mobile Infantry Troop. I was glad that I was not selected.

We were all trained now as far as possible, there would be on-going training when we reached Cyprus and it was published on orders that the Regiment would be moving by train to Liverpool, where we would be embarking on a troop ship. The troop ship was named the *Devonshire*.

The day dawned for our departure from Windsor, which commenced with the Regiment marching through Windsor from the barracks to the station. There was a great turnout along the streets to see us off. When we eventually arrived at the station a whole train had been allocated to us, the families were also going, those that had been allocated Married Quarters.

The journey was uneventful, except for the fact that one or two soldiers went AWOL (absent without leave) during stops at stations, especially at Birmingham. However nothing could be done then, they would probably be caught later. We arrived at Liverpool and boarded the troop ship. I for one had never seen a ship of this size before and I looked forward to the voyage which turned out to be very eventful indeed.

CHAPTER THREE.

CYPRUS

On the 26 February 1956 the Regiment set sail in the troop Transport Ship *Devonshire* from Liverpool en route to Cyprus. We were all warned that we could very well expect heavy seas and gale force winds in the Bay of Biscay.

I for one had no idea where this bay was and, as I had never been in a boat of any description in my life, it was with some trepidation that I settled down to 'shipboard life'. The married men of the Regiment were quartered in the 'families' part of the ship and the remainder including junior NCOs in the sleeping accommodation.

This accommodation consisted of three tier bunks separated by a very narrow corridor. We quickly learned to mark our particular bunk somehow as the layout was somewhat confusing to say the least. We soon settled down to a routine, PT in the mornings on deck and riot training in the afternoons.

Meal times were somewhat hazardous as they were in three sittings. Each man was issued with a different coloured card with numbers on them from one to hundred. When you entered the dining hall your card was clipped. Competition was fierce for these cards so that we could get two meals I still have my sitting card to this day.

Evenings were boring as we were only allowed, I think, two beers from the NAAFI bar. Cigarettes were cheap and we were allowed 140 per week. This turned out to be a problem if you did not get to the NAAFI shop early on cigarette issue day. The popular brands were snapped up leaving only the rubbish brands for those less unfortunate.

The worst of these brands were in an orange packet, the name of them escapes me, and they were terrible, you had to be very sharp when lighting these as they tended to burn away so quickly so as to burn your lips.

Rumour had it that the Army made these especially to try and stop the younger soldiers smoking. They had some use at least as we used to use them as a kitty in the card games that developed in the sleeping space. Everyone knew next morning who had won at cards the previous night as they could not get rid of the hundreds of cigarettes they had won.

After what seemed weeks, but was only about three days, we reached what we were told was the Bay of Biscay. We were drilled in our lifeboat stations and what to expect of the ship should we hit gale force winds and high seas. This turned out to be an anticlimax as the sea was unusually calm and as yet no one had been really ill.

After another day we were told that we were entering the Mediterranean Sea and that we would be anchoring in Gibraltar bay and that there would be some short time ashore. When we eventually arrived at Gibraltar it was a magnificent sight that we saw of the rock.

We were, in fact, allowed six hours' shore leave. Because I had a somewhat misty recollection of a confused boat ride to shore and an even worse boat ride back again I cannot recall too well what happened during that six hours, suffice to say I did not manage PT the following morning.

About a day out from Gibraltar the seas worsened and the sky became a very nasty colour indeed. The storm hit us around about midday and for the next thirty-six hours chaos reigned aboard ship.

Everyone at some point was violently ill including myself, although not as bad as some of the others.

Life below was appalling and the smell of vomit as bad as anything that I have ever encountered before or since. What it was like in the married quarters I shuddered to think, even to this day. In those days those kind of ships were not equipped with anti-roll systems therefore the ship tended to pitch and roll at very acute angles adding to the suffering.

After the sea and the storm had abated we were put to work getting the ship back to its 'pristine' state of cleanliness scrubbing

Christmas 1957. Men of the Royal Horse Guards set off on patrol against EOKA near Famagusta

Johnny Ridge 1956/57

A Sqn tent lines Camp Elizabeth 1956

down the below deck with sea water, drying out damp mattresses and bedding and of course our personal clothing.

This took several days and on the tenth day after leaving Liverpool we docked in Famagusta bay.

We were ferried off the ship in barges and although we were still dressed in khaki the Cypriot winter was cold and wet. I was detailed among others to act as escort to the baggage convoy from Famagusta to our new barracks Camp Elizabeth near Nicosia, the capital.

We had been issued with our own personal weapon, mine was a Sten gun, but we had not been issued with any ammunition. So it was with much apprehension that I and a colleague sat on the back of the open wagon amongst large crates to begin the journey. The wagons were owned and driven by Cypriots and it became obvious from the start that our particular driver had not taken a driving test because to say that he drove erratically was a gross understatement.

We both remained alert during the journey, when we were not trying to keep our balance in the swaying vehicle because the threat of a terrorist attack was not far away, but we were more worried about crashing than any terrorist threat.

We finally arrived at Camp Elizabeth, which consisted of row upon row of large tents. Each tent accommodated four persons. I was allocated a tent with three other mates from my troop. During the next few days we settled into our new surroundings, taking over our vehicles and being briefed as to our immediate role in and around Nicosia.

It was about a week later that I went on my first patrol. We set off in our armoured cars, four to a troop backed up with an armoured personnel car, consisting of six Troop who would be our forces on the ground. Their job was to patrol certain streets of the outer city, the inner city was out of bounds, unless there was a riot. Our job was also to patrol through certain streets looking for any sign of terrorist activity. We also set up roadblocks at strategic places and searched vehicles. My first patrol passed without incident.

The weeks passed quickly enough without many incidents

except that at about that time we lost a comrade. He was killed not by a terrorist bullet but in a vehicle accident out on patrol in his armoured car. His death caused us all a great sense of shock and loss even though he was not in my Squadron. There were to be two more deaths during my stay in Cyprus. These I will describe later.

To give us a rest from time to time we all had to do a stint in the cookhouse as 'Mess Waiters'. It was about six months into my tour that I read orders one day and found myself on this duty together with my mate Pete. The duties consisted of preparing the bread, butter and jam for each meal and serving the same at meal times. Also we were expected to help clean the mess tent and tables after every meal.

As our Squadron was on twenty-four hour call the troopers' mess was opened for the same period to supply meals at odd hours, therefore we found ourselves on a sort of shift rota. We also could be called out to an emergency should this happen and it did on numerous occasions during our tour of duty in the mess.

In those days the cooks consisted of members of the Regiment who had undergone training in cookery. The Regiment had a master chef and in this case it was a Corporal Major Bill Martindale. I remember him as always being dressed immaculately in his cook's whites. It did not seem to matter what time it was or how long he had been on duty he was always immaculate.

Like all senior NCOs in those days they were looked upon with awe and no little fear. However this particular NCO was although very strict also very considerate and helpful. He would not, however, tolerate uncleanliness of any kind in his mess and his wrath was unending if he found an atom of dirt anywhere. I was to meet this man later on in my service and I shall remember him with great affection.

It was during this tour of duty in the mess that I went down with dysentery which was easily contacted out there with the heat and the poor sanitary conditions. Our toilets were of the outdoor type which consisted of a row of wooden boxes with a toilet seat affixed. Each were divided off from the other so that it gave one some sort of privacy.

These latrines, as they were called, were some fifty or sixty yards from my tent and during my malaise I found that I could easily cover that distance in record time when the urge took me, which was very often. I recall an amusing incident concerning these latrines. The Regiment employed several local men to do various duties. One of these duties was to clean out the latrines from time to time.

The method was to remove the wooden boxes and spread quick lime down the trench. This would kill all the bacteria and take the offensive smell away. Well this was the theory. The local workmen, however, had their own way of doing things. If they could they would acquire a jerry can of petrol and pour this down the latrines, small portions at a time and set this alight.

This was done with a second man keeping lookout as this was, to say the least, frowned upon by the Regiment. The second man also had another duty, this was to make sure that nobody was using the facility at the time. On this occasion something went wrong and a soldier had entered the latrine unnoticed and was sitting on the throne when the workman dropped a match down the other end of the latrine.

Fortunately there was very little petrol in the trench, but the unsuspecting soldier beat a very hasty retreat still with his trousers around his ankles. It was rumoured that he was at least two weeks under the Medical Officer, partaking of relevant burn cream. The practice of quick cleansing of the latrine in this manner suddenly ceased.

It was about this time when we were hearing and reading in the press about the extraordinary action of Egypt's President Nasser and the Suez Canal. Rumours were rife, but no one seemed to know what was happening. It began to get more serious when some of our National Service comrades who had recently been demobbed were returned to their Units. More soldiers and equipment were appearing on the island. A battalion of Paras were housed in our camp. These men it turned out were the first into the Suez Canal when the UK invaded Egypt.

My Regiment was of course on full alert to be shipped over with

Amy Helen Georges Me 'Tasty' Ridge 'Cypriot Shop' 1956/57

Members of 4 Troop 'A' Sqn RHG 1956/57

our armoured cars, but to my relief we were not required as the 'War' lasted only some two days. We heard later that one or two Paras who we got to know were killed in action but I never knew their names.

The weeks progressed into months and I suddenly found myself getting ready for my first Christmas away from home. The four of us in our tent, myself, Pete, a chap named Johnny Ridge and another named Taylor had been hoarding our beer ration so that we could have a 'good' Christmas. Fortunately my troop were not on duty over Christmas so we made plans.

Unfortunately Pete was taken seriously ill and had to be evacuated back to the UK. I never saw Pete again until I managed to contact him again just recently and we have plans to meet up again after some forty-three years.

There is a custom in the British Army which, I believe, still stands today, that the senior ranks, officers and NCOs, on Christmas morning go around their soldiers' barracks and take urns of tea to the soldiers in bed. There was always a drop of the hard stuff to go with it as we discovered.

Christmas day duly arrived and we were woken by our troop officer and Corporal of Horse at what we thought a late hour, about seven o'clock, and we duly partook of the 'tea'. We then washed and shaved and settled down to drinking in earnest.

The order of the day was Christmas dinner in the mess at a certain time duly dressed in our best uniform. We would be served a traditional Christmas dinner by the Officers and NCOs and there would be two bottles of beer per soldier.

When the time arrived for us to go to the cookhouse we were all slightly the worse for wear. I remember we all managed to help one another to the cookhouse where we duly ate our dinner and drank the two bottles of beer. My memory is very vague after this. Suffice to say, we were all hung over the following day.

The year had been interesting to say the least only marred by the loss of two of our comrades. The Medical Officer Surgeon Captain Wilson was gunned down by a terrorist whilst visiting Regimental families. His killer was captured by 4 Troop, my old troop, and was convicted and jailed.

The other comrade we lost was a corporal........whilst on escort duty with the Governor's troop. His armoured car turned over at speed and he was killed almost instantly. All three of our comrades were laid to rest in Nicosia's Military Cemetery, their graves have been visited on numerous occasions since.

The new year brought changes to my life in the Regiment. I was posted to 6 Troop, leaving my three mates in my tent and being accommodated in another tent with other soldiers of my troop. I knew these soldiers so it was not too bad a change. I was also now on a countdown to demob as were several other soldiers in the Squadron. We all sported 'demob charts' on our lockers, each day being crossed off as we got ready for bed.

We were called out on numerous occasions to deal with terrorist problems and rioting. I remember one incident when we were on foot patrol. Johnny Ridge who joined the troop later on was with me on this occasion. We were patrolling along a 'waddy' when we decided to have an unauthorised smoke break. We were of course caught by our troop Corporal, Jeff Swann, and as a punishment ordered to recce ahead up a hill where the troop had been ordered to search some old ruins for hidden arms.

We negotiated the hill one on each side whilst the rest of the troop moved up, taking up defensive positions as they went. We surveyed the ruins with binoculars and just as we were ready to call up the troop I thought I saw a movement amongst the ruins. I alerted the NCO and we all got down behind cover. Nothing happened, it was a false alarm. We found nothing in the ruins. I think we all learned a lesson that day.

One night I was involved in a night ambush. These ambushes were set up because our intelligence had found that the terrorists were smuggling small arms and ammunition over the Trudos mountains hidden in local goat herds. Apparently they strapped them to the creatures' underbelly. This particular night I was doing my 'Stag' of two hours when I was alerted by a frightful noise coming from in front of my position where there was a lot of dense scrub.

As, to me, it did not seem an animal noise I alerted the rest of the troop. They all 'Stood To' and the NCO ordered us forward to discover what the noise was. We stopped and the NCO shouted for whoever it was to halt. There was no reply except that there was a furious crashing in the undergrowth. We went forward again and suddenly a furious donkey came charging at us. We, I remembered, scattered and the donkey shot at high speed over the nearest hill. It took me a long time to live that one down.

Another nearly fatal incident took place while I was with 6 Troop. We had been called out at night to a riot in Nicosia. The procedure when leaving camp was to clear your weapon at the gate and load the magazine when on the truck making sure that the safety catch was on.

Unfortunately one of our troop did not make sure his safety catch was fully engaged and with the jolting of the truck a round was discharged as the truck was passing the camp fence opposite the Regimental Orderly Room. The round passed completely through the building without hitting anyone. Again I think a great lesson was learned that night.

It was by now getting quite near my demob so it was with some frustration that whilst reading orders one evening I found my name on the list for a guard duty at a local police station in a small village in the north of the island. This would turn out to be my last duty on the island. The object of the guard duty was to first guard the station from terrorist attack and to patrol the locality both by day and night.

It was on one of these night patrols when I was called upon to make a very important decision. Although only a trooper I was ordered to command this patrol, probably because I was the senior trooper on the guard and because of my experience. The incident took place just outside the village while there was a night curfew. One of my patrol spotted a light off the road so we circled around to find the source of the light.

We discovered it to be a lantern being carried by a local priest. I ordered him to halt in English, Greek and Turkish. I think it went something like this, HALT - STAMATA - DURR. In our standing

TT Devonshire Famagusta Cyprus Feb 1956

Johnny Ridge Pete Hitchcock Camp Elizabeth 1956/57 Cyprus

orders we were required to shout this three times and if the person did not halt then we were to open fire. The priest either did not hear me or chose not to hear me and he continued to walk away.

At this stage, to say the least, I was in a muck sweat. Did I shoot if he did not halt? I shouted again for him to halt, or maybe I screamed, I don't remember. What I do remember to this day my weapon was raised and my finger on the trigger when he decided to halt. I remember my mixed emotions of fear, relief and yes anger, that this man had for whatever reason put me in that situation. We arrested him and took him back to the Police Station where we discovered that he had a curfew pass all the time.

It was coming towards the end of my two week stint at the Police Station and I was getting rather worried about my demob. Other soldiers on demob had left their Regiments and moved to a holding camp to be moved on to UK. It was then, with sigh of relief, when one day a Landrover arrived with my replacement. I remember his name because of a very strange coincidence. Although it occurred well after I was demobbed I feel that it must be told.

The soldier who had come to relieve me was a Trooper Carden. I only spoke to him for a very few moments because I was packing my kit as I was going back on the same transport. Nearly two years later I had met and married my wife and we were on a Easter holiday weekend honeymoon in Blackpool. We were strolling down past the famous tower when I bumped into someone in the crowd. I turned to say I was sorry and he turned as well.

We both recognised each other straight away, it was Trooper Carden, it was really uncanny. He was with his wife and we went and had a drink with them. Afterwards we parted I have never seen or heard of him again.

From the Police Station I was taken back to Camp Elizabeth where I was to see my Commanding Officer for him to say thank you and farewell. The Commanding Officer at the time was Lieutenant Colonel The Marquis of Duro, who has now, I believe, become The Duke of Wellington. I duly was marched in before him and he thanked me for my service and wished me good luck in the future.

It was with much glee that I and my other comrades from my original Squad came together at a transit camp not far away called Wiens Keep, where we would stay until our flight home. Yes we were flying, which caused great excitement as none of us had ever flown before. The aircraft turned out to be a Comet jet flown by RAF personnel.

The actual day arrived that we had all been waiting for two long years. We bade farewell to Cyprus and I for one hoped that I would never visit the island again. Later on in my career I was to see the island again in less dangerous circumstances. We were told that we were to refuel in the island of Malta and when we finally arrived there we had to wait a couple of days as there was a fault with the aircraft engines. We did not see anything of the island as we were all confined to a camp. I was to discover this camp later on in my life when I visited the island on holiday. The camp is now a local craft village.

We took off again and were told that we would land at Southend Airport in the early hours of the morning and that the weather was cold and wet although it was early May. We were all dressed in battledress which we thought would be an advantage coming from the heat of the Mediterranean. This was not the case for when we did land we were all freezing and even colder when we had been transported in a three ton truck from Southend to Windsor.

Our spirits were not daunted, however for were we not getting demobbed. We arrived at Windsor and almost immediately we were 'processed' as they say, each handed a leave pass and rail warrant and told to report back on the 20th June for our demob papers. I arrived home to be reunited with my father and brother. The next day the weather took a turn for the better and the temperature soared to the mid-seventies, however I still felt cold. I got some strange looks from the locals as I walked around wearing a thick sweater.

The leave went rather quickly, the time taken up by buying new clothes etc. and of course looking for a job. I managed to get a job with a local builder who would take me on as a bricklayer so that I could get my trade indentures. I travelled back on the evening of the 19 May 1957 arriving in the early hours. When I arrived in barracks I was ordered first to the medical room to have a medical. You came in 'fit' so you must leave 'fit'.

Next we all took in some items of military equipment, we were to keep a lot of it as we all would have to do three and half years in the TA Reserve, the last thing we were to do was to go to the Orderly Room and receive our demob documents. We were also told that we would receive a letter informing us where to report to our local TA Unit and when.

All the intake had decided to have one last booze-up in the nearest pub before catching our trains home. This we did with some gusto and some time later we all shook hands with one another, swapping addresses and swearing to keep in touch. Sad to say only one comrade kept in touch to this day, his name was Roy Cook.

I walked down Peascod Street in Windsor toward the station, taking one last look around before boarding my train home. I remember thinking to myself, well this is it, I have done my time I won't see this place again. Little did I know that I would be seeing Windsor again in the not too distant future.

Part Two

CHAPTER FOUR

REJOIN AND KNIGHTSBRIDGE

During the ensuing next three years of my life I met and married my wife Mary and we had our first child. Mary was expecting our second child when we both came to the conclusion that working around the area of Shropshire was OK in the short term, but we needed security. As there was no secure job around the area I put it to my wife that I could achieve some security in the Armed Forces. We discussed it with both our parents and they agreed that it was probably a good idea. It was the knowledge that I could sign on for a nine/three-year term that tipped the balance. If it did not work out it would only be for three years.

It was agreed, so I went forth to the local recruiting office in Shrewsbury and signed on in my old Regiment, The Royal Horse Guards. It was explained to me that I would have to wait some time before I could get a married quarter but this did not deter me. Some weeks later I received a letter accepting me in my old Regiment.

Saying goodbye to my wife and daughter was hard, but I braced myself hoping I was doing the right thing by my family and for myself. I set off for Windsor on Tuesday 1 May 1960 arriving before 1600 hours as instructed. I found that Combermere Barracks had been altered considerably during the three years since I was last there. The old block had been torn down and replaced by modern blocks, sleeping six to a room. We even had individual overhead bedside lights, what joy. I discovered the next day that I had joined a training squad two weeks off their pass out. The reason for this I was informed was that I had already done initial training during my previous service and that I was to be the 'trained soldier' for the Squad. My duties were to see that they kept their kit cleaned and up to scratch and their kit laid out in the mornings. I actually passed out on paper.

It was during this period of training that I met a fellow by the name of Ian Ashley, affectionately named 'Jock' and we became good friends. Poor Jock was to meet a nasty end, which I will describe later in these chronicles. I remember one incident in particular, we were 'mucking about' in the barrack room one evening and I had occasion to bang my right knee severely on the corner of the bed frame. So severely that I had to be helped over to the Regimental hospital. The duty Medical Orderly when he saw that the knee was very swollen decided that I was to be admitted to hospital there and then.

I remember that I was in great pain and that I did not care over much where I went. The Orderly gave me a strong painkiller and I remembered nothing until the next morning when I was woken by the daily medical staff. They informed me that the Medical Officer would be seeing me later.

Now, I must explain that the Regimental Medical Officer was a certain Lieutenant Colonel Haywood, affectionately know as 'Jed'. Now this officer was slightly on the eccentric side. For example, I was told a story that a senior rank had occasion to report sick with an unknown ailment. Colonel 'Jed' had run tests on this man he informed him of his opinion of what was wrong.

The senior rank then stated heroically, it must be said, if he could have a second opinion. "Of course you can," commented the Colonel, "I will make the necessary arrangements." In due course the senior rank was ordered to report to the King Edward VII hospital, which was across the road from the barracks.

Upon arrival he was told to go to a certain room knock and wait. This he did and apparently a gruff voice bid him enter and to his horror he discovered that the consultant was Colonel 'Jed'. I never got to know what happened after that, but I was told that the senior rank accepted the second opinion.

But I digress, I lay in my hospital bed awaiting the entrance of the eccentric Colonel. When he did arrive he sort of took the ward by storm. He was a big man, some six-foot plus, ramrod straight, with a shock of white hair. His eyebrows were very pronounced and bushy. He was my idea of the legendary 'Colonel Blimp'.

Full state kit ready for Queen's Guard Knightsbridge 1961

Upon reaching my bed he examined my knee, which was still very swollen and painful. After some consultation he said, "You have water on the knee young man, so we shall have to draw that fluid from your knee." He then proceeded to extract the fluid with a very large syringe and although it was very painful he did it with great gentleness which beguiled his gruffness.

My knee was dressed and I was told that I would have to rest it for a couple of days. This was to me splendid, lying there being waited on, so to speak. However this was about to change. Colonel 'Jed' visited me in a couple of days looked at my knee which he said was normal again, but that my right thigh muscle was soft and needed 'building up'.

He ordered me to sit on the old stove, which was situated in the centre of the ward. This I did, with I might add great uneasiness. The Colonel then ordered a fire bucket to be brought a third filled with water. This the ward orderly did and I could not fail to notice the smirk on his face, as if to say I know what's happening next.

When the bucket arrived the Colonel ordered me to place the handle of the bucket over my foot and raise my leg out straight before me and to continue to do this for two or three minutes. This would happen three times a day, the water in the bucket increased every day. On the third day the Colonel looked at my right thigh muscle and said that he was satisfied. Such was the eccentric humour of the man that he suggested that I might apply the same 'treatment' to the other thigh. When he saw my face he burst out laughing.

"Just a joke, young man, just a joke. However you are fit again to rejoin your troop after you have had convalescent leave." Apparently I was entitled to a day's leave for every day in hospital. I tried to thank the Colonel, but was told gruffly to go and get myself a leave pass and rail warrant.

I managed a fairly quick shuffle over to my Squadron Office and informed the SCM that I had been granted five days' leave. I was told to pack my small pack with the necessary items of kit and report back after lunch. I spent lunch time cleaning my kit to go home in and reported back at the Squadron Office.

My leave pass and rail warrant had been signed so all that was left to do was to book out at the Guard room so I made my way over there. I marched in halted and was inspected by one of the Provost Corporals. He found one slight mark on my belt and ordered me to return to my barrack room and clean it again. I tried to explain that I was on sick leave, but to no avail.

Upon leaving the Guard room it so happened that Colonel 'Jed' was leaving the barracks in his 'car' which happened to be a very old London taxi cab. Upon spotting me, he barked, "You should be on leave, why are you still here?" I explained that I had been ordered back to clean my belt as it was not good enough.

I thought he would take off into orbit, "Who ordered that?" he bellowed. I explained that it was the Provost Corporal. "Come with me," he ordered. We entered the Guard room and Colonel went ballistic with the NCO stating that this Trooper was acting on his orders and that the NCO would not be an NCO much longer, or words to that effect! Sufficient to say I caught my train home for a few days' bliss.

During this period I met the overall training instructor for the Regiment. His name was Corporal Major Bert Humphries, of the Life Guards. This soldier was to my mind one of the most professional soldiers I have ever met. His kit was always immaculate, so was his bunk. He kept all his kit folded and 'boxed' up and he seemed to have two of everything, for it was he you went to if you had an item of kit missing for inspection. A great disciplinarian on parade or on the square and a fair, kindly man off duty. A lot of soldiers did not like him, but my personal opinion was that I felt honoured to have known him and to have served with him.

It was after we returned from leave after pass out that we all would have the option of serving with the Armoured Regiment or volunteering for mounted duty in London. It was during this time that the rioting in Cyprus was rearing its ugly head again and it was rumoured that the Regiment might just be going out again or at least a Squadron.

This put me in a dilemma. I would have dearly liked to go out again to the island, but Mary was pregnant with our second child and I felt that I could not go there and leave her at home not knowing how long I would be there. It was with reluctance then I volunteered for mounted duty. The reluctance in my case was really this. I had done two years on armoured cars and this was the life I knew and liked, the life I knew I could do well in, whereas riding a horse was alien to me to say the least. The old adage when serving in the Army "never volunteer for anything" now applied to me. So, it was with no small misgivings that I volunteered to joined the latest Mounted Training Squad.

The first part of our training began at Windsor itself as we were to do three or four months basic training and then move to Knightsbridge Barracks in London to hone our equine skills ready to pass out as a Mounted Dutyman. Our initial training was to introduce us to the Dutyman's personal equipment. This turned out to be at the outset very confusing. For instance, the khaki uniform was something I had never seen before. The tunic was longer and we wore khaki jodhpurs, which I thought needed a shoe horn to get into, and a long length of puttee which had to be wrapped around one's lower leg at the ankle in a clockwise direction ending up just below the knee, after, I might add one had put on one's boot. When one stood up you felt like a wrapped up pipe cleaner, that is of course if one could stand up.

There seemed to be an art to this procedure which took me some time to master. Another item of kit we were to wear was the forage cap. Although I had worn this previously I had never found it necessary to wear the chinstrap under my chin. Wearing the cap thus prevented the cap falling off when riding. Apart from nearly garrotting me at the least shake of my head, it occurred to me that the Army seemed to protect its kit rather well, to hell with the rider – keep the cap safe.

We were then introduced to the horse's kit both normal and state kit, which at first seemed all too much for me to take in. During the first week or so we learnt how to clean all this kit and to learn the new foot drill. This new drill proved very confusing to say the least. It consisted of one line of soldiers, which when given the

Me Cloaked Guard circa 1960/61 Knightsbridge.

command, right or left wheeled in fours, instead of in threes as was conventional. This drill was really the drill we would use when riding and practising this drill on the ground, so to speak, and it stood us in good stead when we were learning to ride.

In fact this type of foot drill was ordered to be taught to the armoured side of the Regiment later in my career. I remember one such drill parade, it was an Adjutant's Drill Parade on a Saturday morning as was the norm in those days. Each Squadron had been training with the new drill commands for only about a week and this was all too apparent when the first command to the entire Regiment was, "The Blues will advance troop to the left."

It was quite like the start of the Grand National, soldiers seemed to be marching in all directions, except in the correct direction. The Adjutant was tearing his hair out and the RCM was I believe hiding around the nearest wall curled up with mirth. Needless to say this kind of drill was dropped not long after this debacle and the Regiment returned to the conventional foot drill.

Still on the subject of Adjutant's Drill Parades, I did hear a story about a certain Life Guard RCM on one particular Drill Parade when the current Adjutant called the Regiment to attention and ordered them to dress from the centre, this being the command for the mounted Regiment. I believe the order went like this:- The Adjutant - "Life Guards, Life Guards shun. The Life Guards will dress from the centre," pause. Wherein a stentorian voice shouted "Oh no they B........ well won't!!" pause, "SIR". Silence. The Adjutant, "The Life Guards will dress from the Right." Same stentorian voice. "That's better SIR." This story may have been true, I don't know I was not there.

My Squad progressed through riding school at a pace, each week adding more and more kit to wear until we were almost kitted out with full state kit. The full state kit was to be issued at Knightsbridge when we were posted there. The entire kit consisted of the following. You first put on your breeches which were 'Blancoed' white and were skin tight. We wore a special white shirt without a collar and over this we put on our tunic.

This was made of a woollen material with a high gold braided

My 'Pass Out' Knightsbridge Barracks December 1960

neck. Next came the front and back cuirasses with a metal strip over the shoulders, a pigskin strap, also blancoed, held these in position at the waist. A sword was also attached to your waist. The helmet with a red plume attached to it was then placed upon one's head with the chinstrap under your chin.

Last, but by no means least, you put on your jackboots, which were knee high with a pointed 'wing' on the outside. When I first wore this combination I knew how the 'knights of old' felt, the puttees and jodhpurs had nothing on this kit.

I in fact had a panic, one, how the hell was I going to get on a horse, never mind ride it and two how the hell was I going to get off the bloody horse when I could not even move on the ground. I hoped that all would be revealed before this happened. We were gradually introduced to this kit so as to get used to it in easy stages.

I found the riding and the cleaning of the kit a little daunting to say the least, this was not my 'forte' you understand. I had done two years learning all about armoured cars, radios, driving and gunnery, so the world of horses was a world away from the soldiering I was used to. In fact I did not think then I would stay long in this field.

However I stuck at it and finally we were all posted to Knightsbridge to finish our training. When we arrived there we found the barracks to have the basics only, after all this barracks was very old and had not been modernised for some years. Our barrack rooms were situated over the stables and housed about twelve troopers. It had a very small wash house and maybe two or three bathrooms.

It was about this time that the Families' Housing Officer sent for me one day and informed me that there was quarter available for me and this quarter was a hiring. This meant that the Army had rented a flat from a civilian. The rent was paid by the Army and I had to contribute some of this rent from my pay.

I discovered that this flat was situated in North Finchley, some distance away from the barracks. The following week I and the Families' Housing Officer set off for Finchley in a Landrover to take over the flat. In true military fashion this is called a 'March in

Household Cavalry Training Squad May 1960
I am centre rank 2nd from left

or out' whichever the case may be.

We arrived at the location and there waiting for us was the outgoing occupant, who was a Life Guard who was posted to his Armoured Regiment, and his Housing Officer. There were also two civilians employed by the Army to officiate in the handing over of the quarter. One looked after fixtures and fittings and the cleanliness of the quarter and the other all the furniture etc.

As the quarter was equipped with nearly everything you could possibly want it took us about two hours to go through everything, checking for breakages and damages. Everything was counted and ticked off in an inventory book so that everything tallied with what should be there.

There were some minor discrepancies, I recall and these were entered in the inventory and the outgoing soldier was going to have to pay for the replacements from his pay. When everything was completed I signed for the quarter and was told it was now my responsibility.

We returned to the barracks and the Housing Officer advised me to apply for some leave so that I could get my family down from Shropshire. It worked out right as my Squad had been granted a few days' leave to mark the middle of our course. However, before I could organise myself I was ordered to report to the Regimental Orderly room, where I was informed that my wife had gone into labour with our second child and that I was to apply for compassionate leave.

I was now in a panic situation and in a daze I acquired a leave pass and a travel warrant both for myself and my wife. So it was with some haste that I donned my best uniform for the journey home. I was hurrying across the stable yard heading for the Guard room to 'book out' when a loud voice accosted me from the region of the Orderly Room.

"That man there, come here." It was the RCM, a certain Jock Neil. I hurried over and was ordered to enter his office. "Where do you think you are going then?" asked the RCM. I explained that I was going on compassionate leave and why. The RCM looked me up and down, "You will not leave this barracks yet, you are improperly dressed."

As I was standing to attention at the time I could not look at myself for fear of the RCM bawling me out, so asked timidly what was wrong. "Where is your medal ribbon, you're not wearing it?" "May I ask what medal you are referring to Sir?" "The General Service Medal for Cyprus of course," was the reply.

I told the RCM that I had no idea that I was even entitled to one such medal. The RCM then told me that the authorisation for my medal had just come through, congratulated me and told me to report immediately to the tailor's shop and get the ribbon sewn on. The medal would be issued to me at a later date.

I shot across to the tailor's shop and duly emerged with a little ribbon sewn onto my tunic just above the left-hand breast pocket. It turned out that I was the only junior rank in the Squadron that had this medal, so I was justifiably proud.

CHAPTER FIVE

WINDSOR AGAIN

The next few weeks were very hectic. In between getting my wife down and ensconced in our flat I had to do all my training leading up to the passing out parade. On the riding side I believe that I was about average if not below that standard. I had achieved the basic skills necessary, but it became apparent to me that this kind of soldiering was not for me. However, I had a duty not only to my Regiment but to my family, so I stuck at it.

Our instructor was SCM 'Jock' Ferry a brilliant horse rider and instructor even if some of his methods were, shall we say, somewhat unorthodox. It was rumoured that 'Jock' could bring a horse to its knees simply by squeezing his legs together, although I never saw this happen. Well it seemed like that to me at the time especially when we had to ride bare-backed without stirrups or reins, but apparently this was the norm.

My Squadron Leader was a certain Major Darley, who, although being a very professional soldier, had a bad reputation. I was to meet this officer later on in my career.

The days went by with no further incidents that I can recall until the day dawned when we were to pass out of the riding school. I cannot recall much of that day as it went in a blur, getting into barracks cleaning my horse's kit and then my state kit, trying to leave nothing that the inspecting officer could find wrong. We were helped in so many ways by the trained soldiers giving advice and help and we were very grateful.

During our training I had been assigned several horses. This was I was told to get used to the many different horses and their temperaments. I finally landed up with a lovely old horse by the name of Agnes. Let me explain, all the horses that came to Knightsbridge had been trained and were given a name alphabetically, hence as Agnes had arrived with the first batch of that year she was named with the letter A. She was a lovely old horse and had been on Queen's duty many years and I got very attached to her over those few months.

We all managed to pass out that day and as the manpower was at that time thin on the ground we were pitched into the deep end so to speak and found ourselves on Queen's Guard only a few days after passing out. I think at this stage I had better explain about the set-up of a Queen's Guard.

When the Monarch is in residence in Buckingham Palace the Queen's Guard is called a long Guard, when HM is not in residence it is called a short Guard. A long Guard consists of 16 men, consisting of one officer, CoH, and 14 other ranks. These are broken down as follows, four main box sentries mounted, six gate sentries dismounted, three 'chick' sentries dismounted and one trooper acting as a cook. A short Guard was the same except that three main gate sentries were dispensed with.

My first guard went fairly well, although I did not get a very good post due to the standard of my kit, although it was good. The better your kit was cleaned the better post you got, e.g. first relief number one box was the best down to third relief chick sentry. I think I got first relief chick sentry, which, I suppose was slightly below standard.

These guards were, I am afraid, seemingly never ending, 24 hours on, 24 hours off and in those later 24 hours your personal kit and your horse's kit had to be cleaned. There were also stable duties to be done, horses fed and cleaned out and groomed. The only respite came when we had to take the horses down to Pirbright camp for their annual 'holiday' leaving the Life Guards' Squadron to cope with the Queen's Guard. I think I enjoyed my two weeks away from the spit and polish, but this was dulled with the fact that I could not see my family very much.

Whilst on this 'holiday' an incident occurred which could have had dire consequences on my career and my marriage. I had managed to acquire a short weekend pass from midday Saturday until midnight Sunday, so I went up to Shropshire where my wife had taken the children to see their grandparents. I returned on time and when I fell in on the Monday morning parade I found that the parade was also an Identity Parade.

Apparently a young girl had been assaulted in a nearby town which was frequented by soldiers, and she had told the police that the soldier concerned was one of my Squadron, hence the ID Parade. This did not bother me, I thought, as I had been away. Imagine my amazement when this girl picked out me. I was stunned. I was arrested and marched into the Squadron Leader's office, together with the Police, the girl and her parents.

Major Darley asked what I had to say and I told him I had been away for the weekend with my family and that this could be verified by not only my wife, but also by her parents. The Major then proceeded to get his clerk to phone the local police in Shropshire.

Meanwhile I was locked up in the Guard room until some hours later I was marched into the Major's office again. He at once apologised to me about being locked up and told me that my story had been confirmed and that I was free to go. The girl I believe broke down later and confessed she had not been assaulted, or so I believe.

The Squadron returned from our 'holiday' and straight away I was on Guard, once again unable to see my family. It was at this time that I came to the conclusion that this life could not go on for much longer, the strain on myself and my family seemed to be increasing each day.

An incident took place which made up my mind that the life was not for me. I had paraded for Queen's Guard and although I had meticulously cleaned all of my kit the officer inspecting us on the ground (we were inspected on foot and mounted) discovered that there was some dirt in the tiny name on the rim of my medal. I was charged and received two days 'nick'.

I therefore came to a decision to request an interview with my CO and request to be transferred back to the Regiment at Windsor. My request was turned down at first, but due to the difficulties with the strain on my family, which was affecting my work as a soldier, the Commanding Officer sent for me and granted me a transfer back to the Regiment. In retrospect, at the time, I felt that I was letting my comrades down, but I was certain in the knowledge that I was not cut out for this type of soldiering.

My wife was delighted at the news even when I had to tell her that we would have to wait for a MQ in Windsor although I would be allowed to remain in the Finchley flat until a MQ became available in Windsor. A few days later I said goodbye to my friends and 'Agnes' put my kit into a Landrover and set off for Windsor.

I have mentioned my friend Ian Ashley in the previous chapter. Well it came to our ears in the Regiment some time after my departure from Knightsbridge, that poor Ian was dead. There was a piece in the tabloid press to this effect. Ian had been promoted to Lance Corporal and was on the Guard room Provost staff. He had occasion, so the story went, to acquire a pistol from the Guard room and commenced to play 'Russian Roulette' and shot himself through the head. This saddened me for some while and I shall never ever forget him, he was a good pal and comrade.

I threw myself into my new job at Windsor. I had been posted to B Squadron, under the Command of Major P.A. Lendrum, who was nicknamed after his initials PAL (Prolongs Active Life, after the dog food TV advert of that period). The SCM was one SCM O. Price affectionately known to us as Taff, although I never established if he was Welsh or not.

I was assigned to 4 Troop under CoH Jasper Reeves. This Troop was commanded by a certain Lieutenant Parker-Bowles, I was his driver for a short period in Germany. Life was very hectic again although this time I was happier in my work. I was for some months travelling to and fro from Windsor to London daily. At least I was seeing my family more often except when I was on guard and, as these guards only came around about once a month this was pure joy.

I was told at this stage that I was to take a B2 Signals course in Combermere Barracks. I was overjoyed with this as I really enjoyed working with radio sets. This course only took some three weeks and I passed with flying colours. I was to take my B1 Course some twelve months later. I would also take my B3 Gunnery trade at about this time.

Towards the end of 1961 I was informed by my MFO that there was a flat which would be coming available quite quickly in Windsor and that I had been allocated it. One Corporal Woods had been posted to Knightsbridge and would be taking over my flat in Finchley, which I suppose was logical.

I acquired some leave to get my flat ready for the handover and needless to say my wife was overjoyed. At last we would be together, I would be able to go home every night and see my children before they went to bed and see them in the morning before I went back to the barracks.

The day arrived when I was due to hand over my flat. It had been arranged that a three ton truck, supplied by the Regimental MT, would pick up Corporal Wood's boxes etc. take them to Finchley and return with my chattels. Corporal Woods would arrive with the truck, take over the flat and I would go back with the truck. The wives would be travelling by train.

The truck duly arrived and I went to give a hand to unload. The driver undid the tail gate and climbed up inside and to my astonishment produced two long thick planks which he proceeded to prop up against the tail gate, then to my further astonishment commenced to roll down said planks a motor bike and sidecar belonging to Corporal Woods. I managed to hide my mirth and help unload the various crates, placing them just outside the entrance to the flat.

We then loaded all my chattels onto the truck. By this time the various reps and BIAs (Barrack Inventory Accountants) had arrived and we all commenced to hand over the flat to Corporal Woods. All went well and they found no dirt although there were some items of crockery broken. I remember that a bill of £2.10s. was raised against me.

A little apprehensively I signed for this only to be told that this would be OK and that only a very much larger bill would go against me. With some relief I shook hands with Corporal Woods, leaving him in the flat. I never came across Corporal Woods again in my Army career. I duly climbed into the cab of the truck for my journey back to Windsor and for the first time met the driver. His name I recall was Stephenson and because he came from Sunderland was of course called 'Geordie'.

I did not know at the time that this man had a reputation for talking and this what he commenced to do all the way back to barracks and as he had a broad 'Geordie' accent I never understood a word he said so I had to nod my head and make the appropriate sound every now and then. Incidentally 'Geordie' had a brother in the Regiment and they were as different as chalk is to cheese, so much so you would not think them brothers.

We arrived at my new flat to find that Mary and my two children had already arrived. My two girls, Irene, the older, and Elaine were playing in the garden, which apparently was a communal garden for the occupants of both flats. It turned out that we were on the top floor.

The 'March in' went well, the flat was very clean and nothing was missing, the flat was handed over to the BIA by Corporal Woods the previous day. 'Geordie' and the downstairs neighbour, I cannot remember his name, helped us upstairs with all our crates etc.

My family now had our first MQ in Windsor and there were many more to come. I had managed to scrounge a few days' leave so I took my family up to Shropshire again to see her parents and my father. Whilst on this leave I received a telegram ordering me back immediately as there had been a flood in my MQ.

I returned as fast I could to find our flat and the flat below in a terrible state. Apparently a small pipe in the bathroom had burst. This was because the bathroom window could not be closed properly. Fortunately I had reported this to the Families' Officers several times, but the landlord had done nothing. The landlord had to pay for everything.

Not so long after my family's move we were informed on Regimental Orders that the Regiment was to move to West Germany (BAOR, British Army of the Rhine) some time towards the end of the following year 1962. My wife seemed pleased about the prospect of living in another country as she had never been abroad. Thus began another hectic stage in my career, the training and build-up to commence the Regiment's new role in BAOR.

Two or three days each week my troop would be out of barracks training on the training areas near to Windsor and honing our personal weapon skills at the weapon ranges situated in Windsor Great Park. During one of these training exercises I was commanding 'Field Mouse' Scout car (a Ferret Scout car without a turret) and my driver was George Dugdale, who I had met for the first time.

We had been ordered to drive slowly along a road searching for the 'enemy', stopping at each corner whilst I searched with binoculars. If we spotted the 'enemy' we were then to retreat at speed and at the same time report over the radio our position and where the 'enemy' were. I spotted the 'enemy' and ordered George to reverse at speed, directing him backwards.

We had only gone a few yards when I realised that George had passed out and was sprawled over the steering wheel. Before I could do anything we had crashed into a deep ditch and were thrown out. I think I lost consciousness for a short while and when I came to I found George had also come to and extracted himself from the Scout car. Luckily the radio was still operable and we radioed for help. We were both taken to hospital, but I was pronounced OK, but George it seemed had a bug or virus which had caused the fainting.

I was then sent on an armoured car Gunnery Course at Lulworth Camp in Dorset to learn how to fire the main armament in our main armoured car the Saladin.

As I had only fired the 303-calibre rifle and the Sten sub-machine gun, I commenced this course somewhat apprehensively, but with much excitement. The six week course went well and I did well coming about sixth in the class. The top gunner was a chap from my own Squadron, his name was Ted Millichap and because he came near the Welsh border was nicknamed 'Taff'.

Two instances come to my mind during this course. The first was when we were on the firing pad. We had been thoroughly instructed how to deal with a miss-fire. That is to say that when the gunner pressed the button to fire, nothing happened. If this was the case a strict procedure was to be carried out and it went like this.

The gunner was to shout, "Miss-fire, wait one minute." Whereupon the crew waited one minute as timed by the car commander. After this time the gun was re-cocked manually and the gunner instructed to fire again. This usually solved the problem, but if it did not then the next thing was to get the offending shell out of the breech and get it out of the vehicle and up the range where it could be dealt with by the experts. In the Army the definition of an expert was EX is a has been and a SPURT is a drip under pressure.

However I digress, during our next firing session the dreaded miss-fire did occur. The firing pad was cleared of all personnel and the offending shell was duly evacuated from the armoured car and was carried up the range. The firing point officer apparently placed this shell well up the range with the nose of the shell pointed in the correct direction.

He then commenced to walk back to the firing point. Before he had gone many yards the shell exploded. Fortunately the lethal end chose to career up range and because it was an HE round it exploded when it contacted higher ground. A narrow escape.

We were told that this procedure would not happen in warfare, the offending round would just be chucked over the side. One's mind would boggle that if in actual action one would have to stop his car, remove the dud shell, run into 'no man's land' place the shell carefully, and retire.

I duly passed my course and returned to the bosom of my family greatly elated knowing that I would be getting a pay rise now that I had achieved the second of my trades, I was now a Signaller/Gunner, therefore I would get extra pay.

As I mentioned earlier I was also ordered to take a B1 Signals course once again in Combermere Barracks. This was a much longer course, with much more practical training than theory. We also were taught the Morse code and had to be up to between five and ten words per minute to pass the course. I remember sitting up nights in bed with my wife whilst she asked me to recite the Morse code.

I remember always getting the letter Q wrong, quite to the distraction of my wife. At the end of the course we all had to individually open up a Regimental 'NET' consisting of all armoured cars in the Regiment. This was called a 'Forward link'. Also we had to be able to set up a rear link back to the Brigade HQ. I seemed to be able to this quite well so I passed my course, once again with flying colours.

Things were going on a pace now in preparation to going to BAOR. All our vehicles were now being cleaned up and painted ready for handover to the Life Guards' Regiment. Packing cases were issued to individuals and families for packing and returning to barracks to be shipped to BAOR.

Lists of married quarters were posted on Squadron Orders. The address of the MQ allocated to which family and those who did not have enough points would have to wait until one became available in BAOR or until one had acquired enough points. Points were allocated on the basis of length of service, how many children were in the family and how long you had been without a MQ. I had quite a number of points, but I would have to wait.

My wife and children were upset about this, but they were still excited about the prospect of going abroad eventually. The time came to hand over my hiring to the Families' Officer to be eventually handed, I presumed, to a member of the Life Guards. I had arranged for my family to live with Mary's parents until we got a MQ. We were all to get embarkation leave, so I took this and some of my annual leave and spent, I believe, a month in Shropshire with my family.

However before this event the Regiment put on an 'Open Day' in the barracks. This was to let all the wives and families and their relations and friends see how the Regiment worked. There were various stalls and children were allowed to clamber all over selected vehicles and look at various arms and of course the horses.

I remember that my troop were 'volunteered' to take part in an inter-Squadron 'Hockey Match'. We duly took part, not enthusiastically, I might add, as none of us had ever played the game before. I was a soccer man myself and had little if no interest in this 'girls' game. However if we were ordered to play, so be it.

To all the Squadron's delight and surprise we managed to get through to the final. The game was evenly fought in what might be termed as a minor World War Three as the emphasis was on the hockey sticks not the puck. After a rather bruising two halves I managed to score the winning goal by sliding and kicking the puck into the net, disguising this with my stick.

After much shouting and waving of said sticks the referee gave the goal. The troop duly won a crate of beer which was presented by the CO. The crate duly disappeared into the depths of the Squadron block to be shared out.

As drinking alcohol in barracks, other than in the designated bars, was severely frowned upon, I had to devise a way of getting the said beer out of barracks at the end of the day. I have always wondered if the gate sentry heard the clinking of said beer bottles emanating from behind my youngest daughter's pushchair pillow, as we wended our way home.

The sad day came when I had to say goodbye to my family and wend my way back to barracks and await the time when the Regiment left for BAOR. The time came when we handed over our vehicles to the Life Guards' advance party, our advance party had already left, all we had to do then was to kick our heels until the time for our flights.

I was looking forward to the flight, although some of the lads had never flown before so were apprehensive. The day dawned and we left the barracks and headed for Gatwick Airport for our flight to Gütersloh in West Germany. This was to start another episode in my Army life.

CHAPTER SIX

BAOR

We arrived in Germany towards late evening on November 28 1962. Once we had gone through customs we boarded a coach which was to take us to our new barracks which proved to be called Harewood Barracks and were an old Second World War German 'Panzer Kaserne' meaning Tank Barracks. The trip took about an hour and a half and when we arrived we were each told where to find our Squadron block and which room we were designated.

I found my 'bed space' in the middle floor of a huge three storey building. I found the windows to be what would now be called double glazed. The windows had separate 'windows', those that opened into the room and those that opened outward. I unpacked such kit as I had, the rest should be here under storage as it left some weeks ago.

I discovered that I was roomed with a chap by the name of Clive Bell known as 'Dinger', who informed me that the NAAFI (Navy, Army and Ai Force Institute) would still be open and did I want a drink. I was tired from my long journey, but I accepted with alacrity, which proved to be my first mistake in my new posting.

Dinger and several other mates from the Squadron who had arrived with me then set about relinquishing the NAAFI of all of its beer. On arrival at Gütersloh we had been informed that we would be able to purchase duty free cigarettes, but that we would be rationed to 140 per week and that a chit for this amount would be issued when we arrived.

As it was late when we did arrive my mates and I had no chit. However we managed to borrow from those that had been on the advance party. So I managed to acquire cigarettes. We then settled down to serious drinking, or so I thought. The beer of the day seemed to be a beer called AMSTEL, which I gathered was brewed in Amsterdam, Holland.

The favourite seemed to be a drop of lime with this beer and my first seemed to go down well, my second even better and my third better still. I do not remember much after this, all I remember was waking up next morning at reveille with a screaming headache. It seemed that this beer was more potent than English beer. I learned in future to drink this more slowly.

The next few days were taken up with taking over our vehicles and finding out where everything was. Each troop had a cellar in the block where they kept all the troop equipment. We soon found out that this place was a very good place to 'skive off' from time to time. We soon managed to acquire a portable burner so that we could brew up during the day and, although this was officially frowned upon, a blind eye policy among the senior ranks ensued.

Once or twice a week the Squadron had to parade first thing in the morning for PT. One morning, not long after we had arrived, we paraded for a swimming detail to be held in the converted outdoor swimming pool in the barracks. It was, I remember, a very cold morning and we were all shivering when we reached the pool.

We all stood around waiting for the first to 'take the plunge' so to speak. However one of the lads, who in my estimation was either brave or very foolish in that weather, dived in. He was out in a few seconds. "CoH" he managed to stutter, "there is a body down there."

Much to my horror this turned out to be true. Apparently a life guard National Service man, (some had been left behind to finish their service, why I have never found out) had got drunk the night before and had wandered over to the swimming pool and must have fallen in and drowned, a very sad occasion.

I gradually got into the swing of things, a routine within the troop. Mostly training in the Regiment role in BAOR. Our role with our armoured cars was a reconnaissance role seeking out the enemy in front of our main troops. We used to from time to time get 'called out' at any time of the night or day. The Regiment then had a certain amount of time to all the Squadrons out of barracks at a certain RV. Although it seemed to me that when these

B Sqn RHG Harewood Bks Herford 1963. I am 8th from left top rank

particular call-outs came up chaos reigned we seemed to always get out of barracks as a Regiment on time.

I recall one particular Brigade exercise during the winter of 1962/63 when the weather was very bad, the temperatures dropping well below zero and the snow thick on the ground. Half-way through the exercise the Brigade Commander called off the exercise due to this freezing weather. I also recall back in camp a canister of pure antifreeze was kept outside the Guard room during the night. If this liquid began to freeze all the guard were woken and they had to go around all vehicles and start them up, no mean feat, I assure you.

Christmas 1962 loomed up far too quickly and I and many more faced the prospect of spending Christmas without our loved ones and families. Many of the families already out in BAOR invited those personnel who were 'alone' for the festivities to their MQ. I declined these offers as I felt that those families should be with their families not strangers.

Several of my mates and I did, however, enjoy several parties that we were invited to. Christmas eve came along and one of my mates, Bill Borland by name, decided that we would celebrate in style, so to speak. We had managed to save a little out of our pay, which had been put into credits by our pay office. We had requested this money and received it during the week of Christmas.

Bill and I decided, logically, that if we frequented the NAAFI first before we ventured down town we could consume a reasonable amount of alcohol quite cheaply as the NAAFI prices were well below the local 'Guesthouse' prices. I remember we started on beer and graduated to whisky. We decided to purchase a bottle and rapidly consumed this. I remember nothing after this until I awoke in my bed late on Christmas day.

It was in the spring of 1963, after one of the worst winters I have known, that because of my Radio skills I was transferred to SHQ Troop (Squadron Head Quarters Troop). Our vehicles consisted of two six wheeled Saracen armoured cars, Ferret armoured car which was called a 'Field Mouse'. This FV (Fighting Vehicle) had no turret and the crew consisted of the SCM and driver. The Squadron

SQMC would travel with all the Echelon vehicles in their three ton trucks loaded with stores.

The two Saracens were equipped with two radios, one Saracen would be the Squadron's forward link to Regimental HQ and the other would be a link to all the Squadron troops. The Squadron troops would each have a call sign according to which Squadron you were in. My Squadron being B the figure 2 prefixed the troop call sign, e.g. 1 Troop Leader would be 21, 1 troop leader AFV would be 21B, 1 Troop CoH would be 21A and the rear AFV would be 21C.

The Squadron Leader would travel in the Saracen with his operator and he would have the call sign 29, the Squadron 2i/c would travel in the other Saracen and would be 29A, the SCM would be 29B and the Squadron SQMC would be 29F, Charlie not been used.

It turned out that I was to drive the Squadron Leader in the Saracen and double up as a Radio Operator during exercises. I was to remain in this job until 1965, but more of that later. The driver of the other Saracen was a chap called Terry Bennett and over the next three years or so we became very good friends.

It was about this time that we had a tragedy in the Squadron. We had a chap with us, his name I shall withhold for obvious reasons, who had brought his wife out to BAOR and had housed her and his young daughter in a local hotel. This was permitted at that time as MSQs were few and far between. His wife at the time was pregnant and she had become very ill. An ambulance had been called by the hotel, but by the time they had got her to hospital she had died.

The drama had shaken us all for everyone had known this lady and the little girl and of course the husband for some time as he was a well established and popular member of the Squadron. He was granted compassionate leave immediately and his wife's body was shipped back to UK. He reappeared with the Squadron some time later and was granted a compassionate discharge.

Easter 1963 came along and I managed to get UK leave and I arranged to go by train and boat from Herford to Ostend. It was to be a sad journey really, for the soldier that had lost his wife travelled on the same train and boat as me. I remember talking to him about the tragedy, he spoke little of it as I remember, although he did say that not only had he lost his wife but that he had lost all his friends in the Squadron. We parted at Dover and I never saw him or heard of him again, but I often think about him.

I had a marvellous Easter leave reunited with Mary and my girls, who had grown considerably by now. I talked over the matter of MSQs with Mary and we decided that I should look for a suitable hotel in Herford so that we could all be together. The prospect of being allocated an MSQ was remote for at least another twelve months.

Upon my arrival back in BAOR I set about in my off duty hours to find a hotel that was suitable for Mary and the girls. I eventually found one in the town centre and although there were only two rooms consisting of a bedsit for Mary and me and a bedroom for the girls, it was at least something.

The hotel was called the Ritter Stubechen and was run by an ex-German soldier by the name of Deitar and his wife Friedel and their daughter Erica. I returned to this place in 1979 to find the hotel still there run by Erica and her husband. Sadly Deitar and his wife had been killed in a fire some years previously.

I then applied to my CO to live out and bring my family out to Germany. This was granted and the MFO (Married Families Office) informed. They then had to carry out a check of the hotel, this was done and passed. I was then told that I would be paid an extra allowance of 110 DM (about £10) per week to help pay for the accommodation.

I could not get leave so Mary had to fly out with the girls from Gatwick to Gütersloh. They were then transported by bus to the barracks where I met them and took them on to the hotel. At first Mary disapproved of the accommodation as we were, to be fair, rather cramped. But we knew that at some stage we would get an MSQ so Mary buckled down making the best of things. As for the girls' schooling this would come later as they were both under school age at that time.

A few more weeks elapsed and we got into a routine and life for

COH Robson Me Hohne Firing Ranges Germany 1964/65

Terry Bennet, COH Stephenson, Me Exercise Germany 1964 SHQ Troop B Sqn RHG

my family grew better in spite of the cramped conditions. Life also went on in barracks with guards and sporting activities at which B Squadron excelled. We were the best at football and the best on the firing ranges at Hohne. These were I now know the start of the 'Heady Days' for the Squadron which went on for nearly three years. When I look back I think that these years were the happiest years of my Army life.

It was at this time that we said goodbye to our SCM 'Taff' Price who was to be promoted to RCM. We all fell in as a Squadron and Taff was presented with a wristwatch both for himself and his good lady wife. I remember him breaking down as he said his thanks. Taff went on to be commissioned and finished up as Recruiting Officer at Windsor. His place was taken by SCM Johnny Kidman.

As troopers the only place we could enjoy ourselves on a social basis was either down town in the local bars or, as single soldiers, the NAAFI in barracks. It was suggested, I can't remember by whom, that if the officers and NCOs could have a mess why not the troopers. Some of us got together and came up with an idea for having a bar and room in the attic of the squadron Block, which was at that time used for storage and a class room for squadron training.

The suggestion was first made to SCM Johnny Kidman which was met with some slight enthusiasm. He said that he would put it to the Squadron Leader.

I think it was at the end of October or the beginning of November 1963 that an incident took place which was to change my family's way of life for the rest of my service. I was called before the Squadron Leader and told that the Secretary for the Ministry of Defence was making a visit to Herford and that he was visiting soldiers that were living in rented accommodation and that he would be visiting my family at the hotel.

I was told that this visit was to be very informal as the Secretary wanted to see for himself what sort of accommodation the soldiers were living in. I was also told that I would not be present. When I told Mary what was happening she was of course very apprehensive and nervous.

SHQ B Squadron exercise Black Forest Germany 1964 (left to Right) Brigadier His Grace Duke of Wellington, SQMC Jack Cowdrey, CPL Ken Clay, CPL Smith, CPL unknown, COH Jack Peck, myself and Trooper Bennett

When the day dawned I set out for work as usual and I was on edge to say the least as the day wore on. I shot off home that afternoon to find my wife calmly cooking my dinner seemingly unconcerned. My dinner forgotten I asked her how it had gone. Apparently the Minister had arrived early and caught Mary still in her hair curlers. He was followed by the CO, our MO and his retinue.

He had accepted a cup of tea and asked several pertinent questions about the hotel and my family's health. Mary said that she had told him of all the problems that had arisen since we had moved here. The Minister had said that he would try and do something about this problem. I thought that this would be the end of it but I was wrong.

It was a few days after the assassination of President J.F. Kennedy that I was sent for by the MFO, who happened to be a certain SQMC Truslove. I was told that I had been allocated a three bedroom MQ in the town and that I was due to 'March in' on the 29 November. You can imagine my delight, I could not wait to get home to the family with the news. When I broke the news to Mary at first she simply would not believe it and it took me some time to convince her.

I took over the aforesaid MSQ from a SCM Johnny Kidman who had been posted back to Knightsbridge. The MSQ was handed over and I found that everything was laid out and the quarter was immaculate. It was unusual at that time for a junior rank to take over a WO2s quarter, I was not told why, but suspect, even to this day that it was because of the visit of that Minister that I was allocated that MSQ.

The SCM I took over from was in fact my Squadron SCM. We had thrown a party for him as he was a very popular man indeed. He was deemed by the troops as 'one of the lads'. I recall an amusing incident on one of the Regimental Exercises. We had made camp out in the wilds under canvas. It came the end of the day when we all were ensconced in our sleeping bags that Terry Bennett discovered that a ground root lay underneath his sleeping bag.

He got out of his sleeping bag to pull up the offending root, which at first would not budge. Whereupon he gave a mighty heave. Unknown to Terry the root was a surface root and when he heaved the root moved and therefore moved the next person's sleeping bag. This happened to be Johnny Kidman. After some choice words from his lips he then grasped the root and heaved.

The next sleeping bag then moved, upsetting the occupant. By this time the whole tent was wide awake engulfed in laughter. The root now had grown to unmanageable proportions and was causing havoc in the tent. I for one could not get out from my sleeping bag because I was doubled up with mirth. We managed at last to pull up all the root and deposit it outside the tent. It was a long time before all the mirth died down.

Every year the Regiment had to be tested on its Gunnery ability. This took place at Hohne Ranges. I recall on one occasion at Hohne I was taken violently ill, my neck glands swelled up and I could hardly speak or swallow. I went sick and was told rather to the amusement of the medical staff that I had the 'mumps'. Apparently this could be dangerous for an adult. However after a few days rest I recovered.

Our new SCM was SCM Willy Stringer, affectionately known as 'Willy Towrope' although not as well liked as Johnny Kidman, a very good SCM, although strict a fair man. Willy did not stop with the Squadron long, his promotion came through and he took over from Taff Price as RCM. Our new SCM was a different matter indeed.

I remembered SCM Godfrey-Cass from my days in A Squadron in Cyprus, he was a CoH then. When he took over he seemed to change the shape of the Squadron. He was a strict SCM but very fair, he would back you if you were in the right, but look out if you were in the wrong. I remember one such instance. We had been practising for a Commanding Officer's drill parade for some days and when the day arrived I found myself with somewhat of a major problem.

I had cleaned my kit at home, pressed my uniform 'bulled' my boots, polished my brasses and cleaned my white belt. The last item I cleaned was my medal. I always placed my medal wrapped in tissue paper in my pocket of my uniform ready to pin on my uniform when I reached my troop room to change. All the soldiers from the Regiment living in the area were picked up each morning by a three ton truck and driven to barracks in time for 'First Parade'.

This particular morning I caught the truck on time but, however, we were held up for some reason, which I cannot recall. This made us late reaching barracks, but we all still had time to change. Due to this I was probably less fastidious in my preparations to get ready for this parade.

We duly fell in outside our Squadron block and were first inspected by our SCM then by our Squadron Leader. He passed me by with no comment, but the SCM returned to me. "Shortman," he said, "there is something wrong with your turnout." He then inspected me again and found nothing wrong.

Before he could look again the Squadron had to march onto the drill square and form up. As we were the second Squadron it was not long until we were being inspected by the Commanding Officer, the Adjutant and the RCM, followed by our Squadron Leader and SCM. Once again I was passed by all these with no comment on my turnout. Once again SCM Godfrey-Cass had a word with me, "See me in my office after parade," he hissed in my ear. I could not for one moment think of what I had done wrong.

The parade ended and the Squadron marched off the square and we fell out for all to get changed for normal work. As I made my way to the SCM office I chanced to look down at my uniform and to my horror noticed that I had not pinned on my medal. No wonder the SCM thought there was 'something' wrong with my turnout. I dived into the nearest toilet and pinned on my medal in the hope it would not be spotted.

I knocked on the SCM's door and was ordered in. I marched in and halted in the correct fashion. The SCM then proceeded to inspect me once again. He looked at me and said, "I think I know what was wrong with your turnout Shortman, do you?" I thought I had better own up at this stage, "Yes Sir, I was not wearing my

Irene Me Elaine Herford Germany 1964

medal, I forgot to pin it on before parade, it was in my uniform pocket, Sir."

The SCM smiled, "I am glad you owned up and you are fortunate that nobody else spotted it, I won't take any action on this Shortman, you may go, but let this be a lesson to you, always check your turnout before coming on parade." I managed to stutter a thank you and got out of his office fast, very relieved indeed. I never ever forgot that particular lesson.

I think it was about 1964 that the Regiment went to Denmark for a prolonged exercise. We drove up to Kiel, stopped overnight and proceeded next day landing up on the West coast of Denmark at a place called Arhous. We made many friends with the local people in fact several of us were asked out to local people's houses for meals. I liked the Danes very much. The time came to leave Denmark and we were told that we would be doing a long drive to Kiel, which, if I remember was a very long way. We would be starting off in 'packets' (so many vehicles together in convoy) and stopping only to change drivers.

My relief driver would be our troop CoH Jack Peck and I remember we stopped three or four times, finally arriving in the early evening at the German Navy Barracks in Kiel. We were told that we could frequent the German NAAFI and although very tired from driving all day the lads and I from the troop went down and had a good evening drinking with the German matelots. So much so that I finished up swapping my beret and badge for a matelot's jersey which I kept for many years. Incidentally I did have a spare beret and badge.

Another incident I remember during those exercise times. It was during an exercise somewhere in Germany that towards the end of one afternoon we had a message over the rear link from Brigade that the exercise was over. The troop at the time was 'leaguered up' in a farm yard with all the vehicles under cover. The SCM Doug Cass told us that we were allowed down to the nearby village for a few beers. The others and I, namely Terry Bennett, George Murphy and Johnny Midwinter quickly found our bed spaces in one of the hay lofts.

Me circa 1964 Germany

After a meal and a wash and brush up we proceeded towards the village which was only a short distance away. As we were climbing down from the loft we discovered thrown in the hay in a corner the body of a newly born calf, which we presumed had died at birth. Giving this no more thought we all proceeded to get quietly drunk down the village, although not too drunk as we had to drive back to barracks the next morning.

Arriving back at the barn a little unsteady on our feet, we remembered the dead calf and collectively I think, we decided it was worth the risk placing said calf in our Second-in-Command's sleeping bag. The said officer was a Captain 'Crunchy' Crisp, who was fairly well liked in the Squadron. A very fastidious well turned out officer. It was said that he had a set of cut throat razors with the day of the week written on them. Woe betide his servant if the wrong razor was laid out.

We managed with a lot of huffing and puffing to get the said calf up to the loft and sought out the officer's sleeping bag. In our drunken state we managed to get the body into the sleeping bag and then with much hilarity undressed and got into our own sleeping bags. Sometime later Captain Crisp climbed up into the loft and proceeded to get into his sleeping bag. We all held our breath.

Not a thing happened, what a letdown. Perhaps he was, like ourselves, a little worse for the drink. At this time our CoH Jack Peck arrived in the loft, also a little worse for wear. He climbed into his sleeping bag and emitted an almighty shout, the air was blue. In our drunken state we had placed the calf in the wrong sleeping bag.

Jack slept in his blankets that night. We were for the high jump next morning. Captain Crisp seemed to see the funny side of the affair and persuaded Jack to take no action except give us all extra guards when we got back to barracks. I do not think he ever realised that the calf was meant for him and we were not going to enlighten him. Even to this day if I see Jack he always asks me who did the dastardly deed and I always deny it. Sadly at the time of writing this story I have heard that Captain Crisp has passed away.

Time passed on into 1965 and I was reading orders one day when I noticed that there was a paragraph asking for volunteers to train as a Squadron Clerk. It is a well-known fact that most soldiers, at least in my day, had a 'thing' about volunteering for anything. This 'thing' applied to me, but at the time I was getting in a rut, so to speak, and felt I needed a further challenge, so I volunteered. Looking back I am glad that I did for clerking took up most of the rest of my Army career.

CHAPTER SEVEN

Back to UK

I think I was the only one to volunteer for the vacant Squadron Clerk job, so it was inevitable that I got it. So I settled down to a new and demanding role in my Army career. There was so much to learn what with trying to type and trying to take in all the day-to-day running of a Squadron office.

The office was run by George Dugdale an old friend to some degree, now a lance corporal and having done his B3 Clerk's course and heading for his B2, was very competent indeed. In fact George was to teach me many things about clerking and my family and I still retain a friendship with George and his wife Janet.

Most of my duties being an untrained clerk was the job dreaded by most clerks and that is the upkeep of the Squadron filing system. The system at the time was not too complicated because I was only able to see the day-to-day letters in and out of the office. I was not cleared at the time to 'see' anything above routine, Classified and Secret clearance would come later in my career as a clerk.

I had been doing this work for a couple of months when I was told that I had to go on a B3 Clerk's course in Catterick in the UK and as this course was for some six weeks duration Mary and I decided that she should go to her parents for that period. I applied for and got a month's leave to coincide with the course which would be a welcome break for Mary.

In those days as a Trooper I did not get a lot of wages and coming back to the UK I lost my overseas allowance therefore I could not get down from Catterick as often as Mary and I would have liked. I did manage to get down for August Bank Holiday weekend. I fully enjoyed the course, and learned to understand the complexities of the Army system of clerking and the enormous amount of forms that one had to learn.

Each form had a number or code e.g. an Army Form was an AF form and an Army Book was an AB. These letters had a number attached, thus one would know what that particular form pertained to. The one that will always stick in my memory was AF 252, which was a charge report. These had to be filled in when any soldier was placed on a charge for some misdemeanour.

We had to learn to touch-type on the course, which meant that I, because I had been typing with two fingers up to this time, had to learn all over again. To achieve the necessary skill of touch-typing we were all taught to learn the letters, figures and symbols on the standard typewriter. Once we had mastered this a type of screen was placed over the typewriter under which you placed your hands. You then had to type out a sentence using all of your fingers without being able to see the typewriter keys.

We had to practise this procedure every day for the whole of the course, aiming at a speed of just five words per minute. We were tested every day by being given a text to type in five minutes. You were allowed I think five mistakes. I was surprised that I achieved this at the end of the course. However I passed the whole of the course with a high enough mark.

I took my leave of Catterick, glad to see that place I thought for the last time, as it was a dreary place, unloved by most of those thousands of soldiers that had the misfortune to either be posted there or, like me, completed a course there. The next month went all too quickly and it came the time when I had to make my way back to Herford. Mary and I had decided that she should stay for a further couple of weeks.

I had to make my way back via train and boat from Dover to Ostend, so I duly set off about three days before I was due back on the assumption that if the train or boat was unduly held up I would still have time to get back on time. Little did I know that I would be heading into the most embarrassing few days of my career.

The train was on time at Dover and I duly embarked and the ship sailed on time and as it took some four hours for the crossing I duly headed for the bar. I had enough money on me to pay for food and drink and any emergency. In purchasing my drink at the crowded bar, I inadvertently placed my wallet on the bar whilst searching for change and when I looked up my wallet had vanished.

I looked on the floor, everywhere, no sign. I was now very much alarmed for not only was money gone, but also my Army ID Card. I immediately contacted the ship's bursar and informed him of my plight. He was sympathetic and told me this would have to be sorted out at Ostend with the Immigration Police and Military Police, so I left it at that.

Upon arrival at Ostend I went straight to the Immigration Police and tried to explain my predicament. Unfortunately there was no one who could speak enough English to understand me. It wasn't until I said I was a British soldier that I got a reaction from them and they immediately locked me up in a cell, took my cigarettes away, my tie and shoe laces and that's where I stopped for the night.

I was in a high state of fright at this stage of the proceedings and did not sleep very well. It was with much relief that in the morning a Police Sergeant came on duty and he spoke very good English. It turned out that the police thought I was a British soldier deserter and had informed the nearest Military Police who were arriving later.

The police could not have been more polite when they discovered I was not a deserter and they took me out and bought me a huge breakfast and supplied me with countless cigarettes. When the MPs arrived they took my Army details and at once informed my Regiment, supplied me with a warrant to Herford and some money, which would have to be paid back from my wages.

After lecturing me on being more alert on my travels they escorted me to my train. I got a further lecture by SCM Godfrey-Cass when I eventually arrived back in barracks. I learnt a very important lesson from this adventure.

Mary arrived back in Herford and we settled down once again to Regimental life. The attic club had become very successful and had even made a considerable profit since we had formed it. This profit in fact became a problem. There seemed to be no type of account where the Squadron could put this money when we went back to UK and, as this move was now only months away, the problem became acute.

The solution was that as the Squadron could not take the money back to the UK, then the money would be spent in Germany. I think that we all plumped for a weekend in Amsterdam all paid for, including a trip to Amstel breweries and this we did and a good time was had by all.

This was the time in 1966 that the Squadron was to be broken up. The Life Guards were due to go to Malaya and as their Squadrons were to be posted to different parts they required a back up Squadron from the Regiment. Volunteers were called for to make a Squadron and as this initially was only to be a nine month posting I declined to go as I felt that a further nine months without my family would be unfair to them, especially when I did not have to go.

I was dismayed that I could not go to the Far East and when they changed the order from nine months to at least eighteen months I was further dismayed. However this disappointment was tempered by the fact that I was posted to HQ Squadron as Squadron Clerk and was promoted to Lance Corporal, which meant extra pay. The new Squadron was formed and set out for their journey, so I had to say goodbye to some very close friends and comrades.

The preparation for the Regiment's move back to UK continued. The families would be returning first together with the Regimental advance party. Lists were published of MQ allocation and Mary and I were pleased to see that we had been allocated a hiring near Maidenhead. Mary and the girls moved to the hiring in June 1966 and I was to fly over sometime in August. I was very busy at this stage helping with movements of Squadron personnel.

I was also involved at this time with soldiers' passports. There had been an order from MOD that all soldiers were to be issued with a civilian passport. Instructions on how to accomplish this were issued to all clerks. This was a great burden on all of us at this time, in fact the completion of this did not take place until some months after we had returned to UK.

Major Raynor on 'Natanis' 1967

Yacht 'Natanis' Cyprus 1967

A very amusing incident took place during this very busy time as the 1966 World Cup was in progress in England. I was very keen on football and we managed to watch the matches as they came up. This was difficult in those years as there were not many TVs around.

As we all know England reached the final against West Germany. My great friend at that time was Terry Bennett who was living in a hiring near Herford. His wife Anne had just moved back to UK and Terry had handed back the hiring to the German who owned it. The German had invited Terry and one or two of his mates to watch the final on his TV.

When Terry mentioned this I gladly accepted, so we duly arrived at this German's house loaded up with the local beer and watched the match. I was rather dubious at the time as to what the reaction would be by the German if England were to win. I need not have feared as we all had a great time and the German was very kind and considerate about the outcome, if not dismayed over the controversial goal by England. Maybe we made some history there, who knows.

August came around and it was time for the Regiment to hand over to the incoming Regiment, which in this case was the First Royal Tank Regiment. The Commanding Officer of this Regiment was a certain Major Vickers. I mention this for this officer was to be the first Commanding Officer of the Blues and Royals when the Royal Horse Guards and the 1st Dragoon guards amalgamated in 1969.

I handed over the Squadron office and that day flew back to the UK and proceeded on some welcome leave. Mary had got things organised in our hiring which turned out to be on the Maidenhead road some way from Windsor itself. However I discovered that there was a good bus service that would get me into Windsor in the mornings and as the bus station was then situated very near the barracks I would not have to walk far.

I would like to mention the incident that took place just before I arrived back from Herford. When Mary had flown from Germany I had to allocate her sufficient funds from my pay. This took the form of a kind of pension book issued by the Pay office. This book had taken some time to arrive and Mary had run out of ready money. In those days there was no such thing as bank accounts, so she had gone into Windsor to the Regimental Pay Officer to find out what the problem was.

I believe she was told that the Pay Office could do nothing to help her. Of course this upset my wife and angry words were exchanged. At this moment RCM Godfrey-Cass happened to walk into the Pay Office and asked what the problem was. When he discovered that one of the Regimental wives had a financial problem he ordered the Pay Office to sort it out or else!!

He took my wife into his office loaned her £10 telling her to pay it back when she got her book sorted out. Within a couple of days the book and back payments arrived and my wife paid back the loan. When I got to hear of this I asked for an interview with the RCM and thanked him for his kindness. I shall always remember that kindness.

It was during a family shopping trip to the nearby town of Slough that I came across an old comrade from my NS days. We had gone into a butcher's shop and whilst being served who should come from the rear of the shop but Ex WO2 Bill Martindale. He remembered me and we had a talk about the old days. After this I got my meat a little cheaper for many months to come.

Mary and I and the children settled down to our new life, the children to their new school and me to my Squadron Office. It was not long before there was a problem with transport from my hiring. If I remember correctly the buses changed the timings. I brought this to the attention of my SCM and he then asked the MF Office if there was a MQ nearer the barracks as this not only affected me, but some other soldiers as well.

To my delight we were offered a quarter in the barrack area, known as Cavalry Crescent and we all moved there early in 1967. It was a much better MQ and had easy access to the barracks and was very near the shops for Mary and also near the girls' school. Once again we all settled down to our new environment.

During this time I was sent on a first class Army Education

course and as the course took place in barracks I would not be away from my family. The subjects I took were English and Maths and much to my amazement I passed.

It was about this time when a posting came up for A Squadron to go to Cyprus for six months as the Turks and the Greeks were at each other's throats again. I had always wanted to go back to this lovely island again and as I had felt for some time that the time had come for a change of direction in my career this was the opportunity.

I talked this over with Mary and although she did not fancy us being parted again she agreed that I should give it a go. I therefore volunteered to be posted to A Squadron and was granted the posting. I kept my rank of lance corporal and was posted to a troop and became Ferret Scout Car Commander. This meant that I had to learn all about troop tactics and the art of reconnaissance and I only had a few months to learn.

I was learning to command a Scout Car on exercise on Salisbury Plain when I was ordered to set up a roadblock and try and capture the 'enemy'. I found the grid reference and looked for a suitable place to set up the roadblock. I found that there was a high hedge along this road and a little way down there was a gateway.

I got my driver to reverse into this gateway thus hiding the car from the road. Standing in the turret I had a good view of the road without being seen. When the 'enemy' appeared the driver drove the car out onto the road and I claimed a 'prisoner' much to the consternation of the Officer Commanding the 'enemy' scout car.

It was at this time that my career took a blow. Our Commanding Officer, Colonel Redgrave, had handed over to a certain Colonel Mark Darley, who to say the least was a strict disciplinarian. A Regimental ball was organised to celebrate the handover of Commanding Officers. I got the worst for wear and overslept the next morning and was late on parade by a matter of two or three minutes.

Under other Commanding Officers this matter would have been dealt with by the Squadron Leader, but not under this CO. His edict was any NCO who was charged with any offence then he was to be

Barry Lewis A Sqn Cyprus 1967

A Sqn Troop R and R Snake Island Cyprus 1967 (me in foreground)

remanded for *his* orders. I was duly charged and went in front of my Squadron Leader, who was at that time Major Ranulf Rayner, who was I believe heir to the Courtauld millions.

SCM Jack Cowdrey marched me in and the Squadron Leader listened to the charge. He said that I would have just been admonished as I had only one other charge on my records (my burnt battle dress in my NS time). But he had to remand me for COs. I went away fuming at this decision, cleaned my best kit and paraded as ordered. I was duly marched in by the RCM and was demoted back to trooper.

Although I admit that I should have been more responsible I still feel to this day that my case should have been sorted out by my Squadron. This kind of thing happened on many occasions whilst this particular CO was in Command. Unfortunately this officer made a lot of enemies in his time as CO. I have already mentioned this officer in my chronicles of my life at Knightsbridge.

Not long after this incident I was sent for by the Squadron Leader and asked if I would consider becoming his Regimental servant or Batman. I think the thinking was that I should be kept away from the other troopers as I had just been demoted. I said that I would think it over and after discussing this with my wife I decided to try it out.

My duties consisted of seeing that all Major Rayner's personal kit was clean at all times and any other duties that were given to me within the Officers' Mess. The job had its 'perks' one might say as for a start I was excused all guard duties and most drill parades and all Squadron parades, so life became a little easier.

It soon came time to embark for Cyprus and the Squadron flew out on 20 June 1967. We were to be encamped at an old RAF base called Camp Pergamos near the town of Dekelia on the southern part of the island. The summer had just begun and we were all warned about the heat and contacting sunburn, which one could easily do if one was not careful. Luckily I had a certain amount of experience as I had served some time on the island.

I had not been on the island long when Major Rayner approached me and asked if I would mind looking after a yacht

Me on Natanis Cyprus August 1967

belonging to the Regiment which was moored in Kyrenia harbour in the northern part of the island. Although I knew nothing of sailing or yachts it turned out that Lance Corporal McGuiness was to help me as he knew something about sailing. The yacht was named *Natanis*.

The yacht was to be used for the purpose of Rest and Recuperation for all ranks of the Squadron for the duration of the Squadron's stay on the island. The idea was that Major Rayner would actually sail the yacht (with the help of whoever was on board) out to sea and around the island. Lance Corporal McGuiness and I were to stay on board for the duration to look after the yacht.

It was the beginning of the most joyous time in my career. We had all the facilities on board and our rations were brought to us each week, including our pay. We had the facilities of a rubber dinghy with an outboard motor and the use of snorkelling gear and scuba gear. (Diver instructors were available at any time.) Life became almost idyllic. We were always dressed only in shorts and with little to do in the maintenance of the boat we had plenty of time on our hands.

It was at weekends that the soldiers from the troops came over to spend two or three days with us. This proved very exciting and worthwhile. Mac and I learned to handle the boat increasingly well, learning about sails and the way to turn with the wind. An amusing incident took place on one of our trips. We used to tow the rubber dinghy behind us so that when we dropped anchor offshore we could get ashore if need be.

I remember that I was at the tiller when I noticed that the dinghy had come adrift and was floating away behind us. I alerted the Major and he at once took the tiller and we commenced to try and come around. This is always a difficult manoeuvre, especially with a learner crew. The dinghy was getting further and further away from us as we were trying to get around. The Major asked for a volunteer to dive over to swim for the dinghy and get the engine going so that we could get it back that way.

I don't know why but I suddenly found myself diving overboard and striking out for the dinghy. Fortunately I have always been a strong swimmer so reached the dinghy without mishap. Unfortunately I could not for the life of me get the outboard motor started. So I had to row for it. By this time the yacht was some distance away and I seemed not to be making any progress. It was very difficult I remember for there were no seats in the dinghy, so I had to kneel to row.

I was beginning to panic somewhat when I noticed that the yacht had come to a stop as the Major had seen the problem and decided to stop with the bows pointed in my direction. I still could not get any nearer as there was probably a current somewhere. I rowed on and looking behind to my relief the Major had set sail again to close the gap so it was not long before I managed to get back on board. Looking back on this incident now I could have been in some danger, but I did not think about this at the time.

They say that when you are enjoying yourself time goes quickly and so it was, we were coming to the end of our tour on the island.

But before we got ready for our move two more incidents took place. The first was peaceful enough. The Major had decided to buy an orange grove near to Kyrenia and he asked for volunteers to plant the orange trees so we were put to work planting, what seemed to us, an enormous amount of orange saplings.

Just as we were finishing this job an emergency came about. The Turkish nation, always disputing the ownership of the island, decided they were going to invade. The Squadron was put on full alert and were ordered to get all the UK civilians and families into the camp area and house them as best we could whilst the emergency lasted. Mac and I were recalled from the yacht to help with this problem. I, as a trained clerk, was put to work on the enormous amount of paper work involved in moving all these families out of their quarters.

We were all told that the Squadron would not be going back until this was resolved. The Squadron orderly room set up a telegram system where married soldiers could telegraph their wives to reassure them we were all OK. I duly sent my telegram off. The emergency did not last long as the UN stepped in and negotiated a peace of sorts.

Our relief Squadron duly arrived to take over the problem of getting the families back into their quarters and the Squadron departed for UK. We arrived back in UK on 12 Dec 1967 having completed a memorable, to me, six months' tour. I would not have missed it for the world. When I did get home to see my family Mary was most upset that I had not sent a telegram as others had done.

I assured her that I had done and the telegram must have got mislaid. I don't think at the time that Mary was completely satisfied as to this explanation. It was only the following day that my daughter brought up a telegram to our bedroom, it was the missing telegram. It had taken some three weeks to arrive.

I settled down to life again in UK still 'Batting' for the Major. This was to go on until his resignation from the Army. The Regiment was now told that it would be amalgamated with the First Dragoon Guards sometime in 1969 and that then we would be going to Germany again, but we were to be trained as a Tank Regiment. I, for one, did not relish this amalgamation for various reasons so I began to think seriously of coming out of the Army when my nine years were up, which was in early 1969. My decision was to play a great part in the next phase of my career.

Part Three

CHAPTER EIGHT

DEMOB AND TRANSFER

Life became tedious for some time after the excitement of Cyprus. I was still 'Batting' for the Major and this carried on through the remainder of 1967 and at the start of the year (I believe it was) the Regiment was told that it would be moving down to Perham Down near Tidworth in Hampshire to commence training on tanks.

Life was never dull for too long so my family and I started to get ready for another move, acquiring packing cases and deciding what to pack now and what to leave out. Another thought was the girls' schooling. This was done mainly by the Families' Office, they advised where the schools were and when to go and see them.

As we were moving around August it would be just right for the girls to leave their old school and join another after the summer holidays. It was about this time that Mary's mother and father came down to spend some time with us, so we decided to hire a car and go down to Tidworth and look at the girls' new school. We did this the day before I was to take Mary's parents back up to Shropshire. We had a good day, the girls had a look around their new school and liked what they saw. We also had time to look at from the outside the brand new MQ we had been allocated.

It was on the way back that disaster struck. A stone from a passing lorry totally smashed the windscreen and I drove back to Windsor with no windscreen at all. This posed a dilemma. I knew that I would not have time to get the windscreen repaired before the next day and my father-in-law could not stay on as he had to be back at work. I managed to get the windscreen replaced at home.

I rang the hire firm, they were sorry but they had no other vehicle available. I would have to get it repaired as there was no windscreen insurance in those days and I would have to make do.

We set off the following day dressed in winter clothing although it was quite a warm day. We managed somehow to get all the way home and it was the most uncomfortable drive I have ever had.

It was getting near the time for the move and the Officers' Mess decided that they would have a 'going away summer ball'. I volunteered for this because you got extra pay for this duty, paid by the officers. Our duties that night varied from receiving the guests and taking their coats at the main entrance to serving drinks and helping behind the bar.

I remember that I was behind the bar and was rushed off my feet for most of the evening. Now whether it was the custom or not, I do not know, but it seemed that every officer that came to the bar and other guests were buying me drinks. I was told that if this was the case then I was to put the equivalent money not in the till but in a separate receptacle. This I did but managed to have a couple or so drinks while no one was watching.

At the end of the evening when all the guests had departed, this was about four or five o'clock in the morning, the CO came to thank us all for our 'Splendid efforts' as he put it and said there were some drinks for us in the back room of the mess. Cheered by this offer from our not much liked CO we set about drinking the free beer.

By about five thirty or six I remember I was slightly the worse for wear so I wended my way home. I must explain that we had to wear our 'Blues' uniform for this ball. This consisted of very tight trousers over riding boots with spurs attached to the heel. The jacket was long with a very high neck. When I arrived home trying to be quiet so as not to wake the family I managed to get my jacket off. I now had to negotiate the stairs and bearing in mind my state of intoxication and what I was wearing, this proved too much for me.

I managed the first three steps then for no apparent reason my spurs got crossed and unable to proceed I lost my balance and crashed full length on the stairs making such a noise it woke the household. My two girls arrived first on the landing and seeing my plight proceeded to very nearly fall over laughing. I was not amused at the time.

Mary then appeared and she too was very amused. After a lot of huffing and puffing she and the girls managed to get me to my feet and into the bedroom. It was now that I realised that I would have to get my tight trousers off, a difficult job when sober, a near impossible job in my state. I therefore decided much to the consternation of my wife to climb into bed still clothed. This of course did not go down well with Mary in the slightest so I had to sleep in the chair downstairs and it was a good job it was Sunday.

Came the day that we had to move to Perham Down and we knew it would not be long now before my demob as I had decided to try civvy street once again. The Regiment had frozen all promotion in readiness for the amalgamation and I felt ill at ease with this decision.

I did not think that my future lay in this situation. A few of us had applied to transfer to the Life Guards rather than be amalgamated with another Regiment. We felt that the Regiment would be losing its identity. Some soldiers were granted their transfer, but I and many more were not. This decision by our CO finally made up my mind to go out.

A sad day came just after Christmas 1968, Major Rayner had decided that enough was enough and resigned his commission. I had been his servant for just two years and he had always been kind to me and treated me as an equal when off duty. He knew that I would be leaving the Army soon after him so he called me into his office one day and out of the blue offered me a job as his servant when I got demobbed.

He said that he would be going around the world promoting Courtauld's products, and as I had been a good servant to him he would like me to go along. This seemed a fantastic offer and I asked him if I could think it over.

I went away to discuss this offer with Mary and the girls. When I got to thinking this over Mary and I came to the conclusion that though I would like to be able to work for a good boss, going around the world without my family was not on, so with some reluctance I told the Major I could not accept his offer.

It was not long after that he left. I took his suitcases and luggage down to the local station and saw him off. Just before the train pulled out he pressed an envelope in my hand saying that this was my Regimental pay, wished me luck in civvy street and the train departed. I have never seen this gentleman again.

When I got home that lunch time I opened the envelope expecting my two pounds monthly Regimental pay, but to my surprise there were five crisp ten pound notes together with a short note wishing me and my family well. Fifty pounds in those days was a small fortune and this would help me and my family to settle down once we had moved.

It was about this time that Mary imparted to me the wonderful news that she was pregnant. It was wonderful because we had been trying for some time for another child for we both wanted a son. The girls seemed excited about it as I think they both secretly wanted a brother too.

I had got to the stage now where I had organised a demob course of my own with a local haulage firm in Oswestry, where we intended to live. I was to see the CO prior to my course and move my family at the end of March 1969, complete my month's course and return for my demob papers at the end of April.

Everything went smoothly at first and I was marched in front of Colonel Darley for the last time I thought. He gave me a short lecture on keeping up my standards in civilian life and I was marched out. I had arranged to hand over my MQ and hired a small van to get my possessions up to Shropshire as the heavier stuff had already gone by rail.

On the morning of my 'March out' disaster struck. Mary came downstairs with a very severe nose bleed. We could not stop this so I managed to get her over to the Regimental Medical room, which was fortunately very near. With all their efforts they could not stop the bleeding and she was losing a great deal of blood. They rushed her off to the Tidworth Military Hospital.

I rushed back to the MQ and gathered up the girls and deposited them with our next door neighbour then rushed over to the orderly room. Fortunately RCM Godfrey-Cass who was there saw my consternation and discovering the problem rang the BIA Office and cancelled the 'March out' indefinitely. He told me to wait as the CO would want to see me.

A few minutes later I was marched into the CO's office and I politely informed him of the problem and requested permission to remain in my MQ until such time as Mary was well. He granted me permission to stay in the MQ, but to the RCM's and my utter amazement he insisted that I go on my demob course in Shropshire and would listen to no excuses.

I am afraid I lost my temper with this officer to the extent that I told him exactly what to do with the demob course and that I was not going on this course as I had no one to look after the girls and that I certainly would not be leaving my wife in hospital. I was marched out hurriedly by the RCM. He told me to go home and see to my family and that he would deal with it. I heard later that he managed to persuade the CO that I was right.

It was touch and go with Mary for some three days, but to my relief she pulled round and quickly began recovering. I had not gone on my course. I had rung the firm and they had cancelled the course and told me to arrange it another time.

It was nearly a month before Mary was well enough to travel and during this time I was overwhelmed with best wishes from friends in the Regiment including many senior ranks and officers, the RCM among them. He in fact came to my home on several occasions to ask if there was anything I wanted. I noted that the CO was not among the well-wishers.

The time came to take my leave of all my friends and the Regiment. I did this with great sorrow as I loved my life with this Regiment. I was also angry that I had to make this decision, angry with the people that had deemed fit to amalgamate a splendid Regiment that had done its duty in numerous wars and battles.

For over three hundred years the Regiment had served its Kings and Queens with honour and bravery. I am sure that the Regiment it was amalgamating with had done equally well in its history, and that soldiers from their ranks were equally dismayed with this amalgamation.

My wife I had discussed our future and we had agreed that I should at least try 'civvy street' for a while to see how we got on. We managed to get a home and I got a job, but it was after only a few months that I felt that this was not the life I wanted.

I was more determined now to go back to Army life, but not in the 'Blues', I wanted to be in the Life Guards. I somehow knew that life back in the old Regiment would not be the same. I was proved right and I will explain later on in these chronicles. I hit upon a plan – what if I signed on in the Army in a different Regiment and later transferred to the Life Guards?

Life went on for some months until joy of joys Mary gave birth to a baby boy and we christened him Andrew Peter. He was born on my eldest daughter's birthday, exactly ten years to the day. I remember that when I told my two daughters that they had a brother, they were not too pleased, their comments being, "I suppose we will have to babysit now."

Mary and I then talked over our future and came to the conclusion that the best course of action was to put my plan for re-enlistment into operation. With this plan in mind I went to my nearest Recruiting Office. I did, of course, have to inform the Recruiting Officer that I had been in the Army before and they of course tried to persuade me to rejoin the old Regiment, but I was adamant that I wanted to join another Regiment or I did not rejoin at all.

I had thought about the problem of which Regiment. It was really all about simply choosing any Regiment. I plumped for the Royal Artillery. So I signed on in the Regiment and in due course much to my amazement and to that of the Recruiting Officer, I was accepted and was duly posted to the RA's depot at Woolwich, in London.

I arrived there and after a lot of interviews with various officers as to what I should be trained as if not a Gunner. I was posted to a camp called Barton Stacey, which I believe is in Wiltshire, to what was called the 16th Light Artillery Regiment. I had been informed that as I had quite a lot of service completed that it was probable that I would get a MSQ quite quickly. I was then kitted out with complete new kit and issued with a rail warrant for my journey.

After a long train journey and being picked up at the local rail station in a Landrover, I arrived at the camp. I was tired from this journey and the sight of the camp did not lighten my spirits. It was then that I began to wonder if I had made the right choice in Regiments.

The camp consisted of old Nissen huts which were new, maybe at the start of the Second World War, with a sort of road around them leading to, I assumed, other huts of a similar type. I saw no sign of MSQs. Maybe they were elsewhere, I hoped. I duly booked in at the Guard room and was told to report to the Regimental Orderly Room and was directed to it.

The Chief Clerk took all my papers and directed me to my living quarters, which was, yes, a Nissen hut. I enquired from him where the Families' Office was and I went across the camp and after getting lost several times because each Nissen hut looked the same to me, eventually came across a hut marked Families' Officer.

The FO turned out to be a senior NCO and after listening to my request for a MSQ explained that there were in fact some quarters available at the back of the camp and that it seemed that I had enough points to qualify for one. I did not believe my luck, that is until I saw the quarter that was offered. Yes! A *Nissen hut.*

I did in fact look inside and they were quite nice and well equipped, but I could not see my wife being very enthusiastic about a hut. However I told the FO that I would ask my wife about it and gave the excuse that she may want to stay where she was for the time being. This decision was, in fact, taken out of my hands the very next day.

By asking around and once again getting lost within the maze of huts I found my Battery office. This I did so as to read orders for the next day. I discovered that I was to be marched in to see the Commanding Officer. I cannot recall making any friends during this stay. I remember having a few beers in the camp NAFFI (Nissen hut again) and getting up for parade the next morning.

I duly paraded for CO's Orders the following day and was marched in before him. In no uncertain terms he told me that I would not make a good 'Gunner' and would I like a posting as a brigadier's servant to the officers' training camp at Sandhurst. This was because I had let it be known that I wanted a transfer to the Life Guards and this was obviously on my records.

This decision I did not have to think about. I told the CO that I would like this posting. He agreed and wished me well and I marched out. The RSM told me that I would not be required for any duties and that I was to pack my kit and be ready for the posting.

I used to ring my wife two or three times a week at an agreed time at her local telephone box (no such luxuries as one's own telephone in those days). So I rang her that evening and told her of the events of the last two days. She seemed very amused at the prospect of living in a hut, she never saw them!

The next morning after breakfast a corporal appeared and told me that the RSM wanted me, so I went across to the Orderly Room. I only got lost twice this time, maybe I would get used to these huts after a year or so. The RSM informed me that I would be going to Sandhurst that afternoon and to be at the Guard room with my kit. The Chief Clerk issued my posting orders and I was once again on the move. I had a secret feeling that they wanted this 'ex Guardsman' away as soon as possible.

I arrived at Sandhurst Officer Academy, booked in at the Guard room and was sent across to the Orderly (once again) where I was told where my accommodation was. This consisted of an actual barrack block (thank God not a Nissen hut) where I met some chaps who were in the Royal Corps of Transport.

Most of these chaps were drivers assigned to officers to drive them from place to place in staff cars. I settled in and paraded next morning with everyone else. I was told to report for CO's Orders at midday. Upon marching into his office he greeted me and told me that I would be looking after a brigadier, who was Deputy Commandant of the Staff College.

This part of Sandhurst was a College for Officers from all Regiments of the British Army and those of other Armies throughout the world. The Brigadier was a Brigadier Bethall, funnily enough an old Royal Artillery man, who had served in the last war.

It was not until several years later I was to discover that this officer had been captured in Italy and had escaped and found his way back to the British lines. He in fact made a documentary TV film with his two sons showing them his escape route.

I was eventually shown into his office to meet the man himself. He was a very tall man and every inch an officer. He sat me down and explained to me what my duties were to consist of. To my delight he also said that there was a cottage near to his officer's MQ where my family could be housed. He then sent me off to organise my family's move together with a few days' leave.

As it was a furnished MQ I left some of our own furniture in store for the time being and the Brigadier kindly lent his own van to transport my wife and my three children down from Shropshire.

Life settled down. I alternated between the Brigadier's house and my cottage. My duties included helping the lady who looked after the household chores, but mainly my duties were cleaning the Brigadier's Army kit i.e. brasses and pressing shirts and uniforms etc. For this task I had a cleaning room to myself with all the necessary equipment I needed.

Our next-door neighbours were a couple named Ron and Daphne Jenner who had two daughters roughly the same age as my two. We all got on well together. Now Ron was a fine wine maker, not only fruit wines but also root wines. He had a large supply of wines that he had made over the years. I got interested in the art of wine making and Ron and I spent many an hour experimenting with various wines.

One weekend we decided that because I had three apple trees in my garden and they were overloaded and they were cooking apples, we would try and make a large quantity of cider. Both families got involved and we picked a large quantity of apples. The problem then was how to squeeze the juice out of them. The problem was solved by simply cutting the apples into small pieces and putting these through a mincer.

This process took most of the weekend, but in the end we managed to acquire nearly five gallons of what looked like an evil concoction. We added the necessary sugar and yeast, covered up the container, placed an air lock in the lid and placed it in a suitable warm cupboard near Ron's heating system. After about three days this concoction was bubbling away furiously. After a further three weeks and several agents we had added, the cider was ready to sieve. We completed this process and then sat back to wait until Ron was satisfied that it was ready to drink.

Towards the end of the summer on a warm Saturday afternoon Ron asked me to give him a hand to grub up an old tree stump in his garden. I readily agreed and worked all afternoon. When we had finished Ron suggested a cool drink and why didn't we break open the cider, just to taste you understand, said Ron to his wife and mine. This we did and and having had just one glass which we all said was very good, we all retired to our own dwellings. I don't remember much after this, but my wife swears to this day that I was completely incoherent most of that evening. It goes without saying that Ron and I did manage to finish off this lethal brew, but it took us very much longer than was anticipated.

As we came towards the end of the year I met up with an old friend, George Dugdale, who was on a course locally. He was at the time the Life Guards' Orderly Room CoH and he and his wife Janet and Mary and I went out a few times with them to dinner and a few drinks. I broached the subject of me transferring to the Life Guards and George said he would have a word with the RCM and Chief Clerk.

It turned out very well and the Life Guards would accept me providing the Royal Artillery would be in approval. I at once broached this subject to the Brigadier who said that he would, though reluctantly, see what he could do. He told me that he may be posted to another job and that he would like me to go with him. It was left at that for the time being.

I carried on with my duties whilst this matter was being resolved. Over the months with the Brigadier I had been asked from time to time to 'wait' at table when the Brigadier threw dinner parties. It was at one of these parties that a very embarrassing event took place. I was serving on, I think there were about eight around the table and I was serving the vegetables. I had already served the meat. The vegetables consisted of potatoes in one dish and red cabbage in the other, one in each hand.

I had just served the Brigadier's wife and in turning the corner of the table the dish with the red cabbage on decided to go in the opposite direction. The dish hit a nearby side table, hitting a table lamp on its way, and scattered its contents up the very elaborate wallpaper before coming to rest. The silence that ensued was deafening. I made my apologies, went to the serving hatch and asked for more red cabbage. What else could I do? I finished off the dinner and the guests went into the drawing room where I served the coffee.

I then went back into the dining room to try and clean up my error, only to find the General's wife and the Brigadier's wife cleaning up for me. I was, to say the least, very embarrassed but both the wives were very gracious about it and although the Brigadier was very angry about it, I got no dressing down from him. In fact the General took me to one side and told me he thought it was very embarrassing for me and not to worry about it.

Just after Christmas of that year I received the OK from HQ Royal Artillery to go ahead with my transfer to the Life Guards and in March 1971 handed over my cottage and sent my family back up to Shropshire. The reason I did this was because the Life Guards were going to Germany in August and it was rather pointless setting up in MQs in Windsor just for a few months. Once again this move began a new and varied chapter in my Army life.

CHAPTER NINE

WINDSOR, GERMANY AND NORTHERN IRELAND

On 21st of April 1971 I travelled to Windsor once again to take up my posting to the Life Guards. Upon arrival I reported to the Orderly Room and was ordered to the QMs stores to be rekitted out in a new uniform, headgear and badges. I was also informed that I was to go to HQ Squadron for the time being.

I duly reported to HQ Squadron office and was told that I would be seen by Squadron Leader Major J. Fuller the following day. I found myself a room in HQ Block and settled myself in, got myself cleaned up and booked out of the Guard room for a night out in Windsor.

The next day I was marched in front of the Squadron Leader. He greeted me and told me that he thought that as I had a very good service record, I would be, he thought, a great asset in the Technical Quartermaster's troop, and what did I think? I said I would do my best and so it was to be the start of a long and enjoyable time in this troop.

I got changed out of my best kit and went down to report to the Quartermaster (E) as he was called (his equivalent in the Royal Horse Guards was Quartermaster Tech). At the time it was Captain Jim Greaves who was at one time the RCM of the Regiment. He was nicknamed 'Jumbo' I never did enquire why this was so.

He welcomed me to the troop and introduced me to his staff. The TQ being WO II 'Kiwi' Howells and the Office CoH was Bill Hatto who would soon become HQ SCM. On the tech side, which I will explain later were, SQMC Don Johnson, Corporal Bill Bourne, LCoH Gerry George and Trooper Charlie Harrison and Trooper Vince Trench.

I was to be the office clerk and I was to get to know the ins and outs of all aspects of the troop work. Let me explain. The troop supplied all technical stores for the whole Regiment i.e. weapons, transport and all necessary parts for all these things. It did not supply clothing, bedding or accommodation materials, this was done by the other Quartermaster. We were known as QM 'Nuts and bolts' while the other QMs were known as 'Boots and Socks'.

I spent a little time working in the various sections of the troop to get to understand the way the troop worked and was organised, but my main duties were the office duties, which consisted of filing, typing letters for the QM and seeing to the mail in and out. The mail out was mostly demands for all sorts of stock from the smallest screw to a radio set, for as one item was issued out it had to be demanded from Ordnance stores to replace it, so that the numbers of that particular item were kept constant.

The time wore on when we would be moving to Germany to a place called Detmold, which was not far from Herford where I served with the 'Blues'. The Regiment was to take over a barracks called Lothian Barracks and we were to move in August 1971. I had registered my family with the Families' Officer and as the Regiment got nearer the time lists appeared on the Squadron notice board where our families would be living.

As I was to be on the main party my name came up at last. I was to move to an estate in Detmold called Hakadalh and my family and I would be on the top floor of a three storey block. I eventually got leave and I went up to Shropshire and spent some time there and then brought Mary and the children down to Gatwick airport on 20 August 1971 where we flew to Gütersloh and were then transported to Detmold by bus.

The children's school had been sorted out beforehand. The girls were to travel each day to Gütersloh and Andrew, as he was only two was to be at a local school when he reached the age. We found the flat very clean and tidy and commenced to unpack our cases and settle in. Our main crates would be arriving at a later date but as the quarters, in those days, had everything one required issued, we had few of our own belongings.

I reported to the barracks the next day to find my troop was housed in a very large building at the rear of the barracks and on the second floor. Access to this was up a very steep ramp. Housed up there were four three ton trucks, which housed thousands of items of spares, two trailers, one office trailer and one sleeping trailer, these to be used when on exercise in the field.

As the Regiment had been trained on Chieftain tanks for some time before I joined it, I had not seen one of these vehicles except in pictures. The Regiment had some forty-seven of these monsters, therefore the troop had a tremendous amount of spares and equipment, more than we had in Windsor. So we had to learn all over again.

This was at the time a part of Regimental history. As the Regiment was to be sent to Northern Ireland the next year as part of an Infantry force, the Regiment would be deployed on foot for the first time in its history and it would have been involved in three separate roles in twelve months, an Armoured Regiment, a Tank Regiment and a Foot Regiment. I was rather proud to be part of this unique achievement.

I settled down to my work in the Tech Office and I was to work with a LCoH Sid Brandon, who was a Blue and Royal, having been a Royal when the two Regiments amalgamated in 1969. He had been left in Germany simply to finish off his time as a regular as he had chosen to remain in Germany after his discharge. His wife was German. He proved to be invaluable in his knowledge of the way the Regiment worked and the way the troop worked. He taught me a great deal.

One of my many duties was to keep an account of all vehicle mileage, especially the tanks as these were restricted to a certain mileage each year. I had to submit these figures to the Regimental Second in Command each month, who at the time was Major Gouch, whose father had served in the Regiment, who was a stickler for preciseness. I had to be very much on the ball as he would ring the office and ask not only for the monthly figures but the figures for the current year. It was always difficult the collection of these figures for one main reason.

TAC HQ LG NI 1972 Tpr Burke, LCPL Donavon, LCPL Shortman, LCOH Dickson

Me Ops Room Mount Pottinger Police Stn Belfast Nov 1972

I issued mileage proformas each month to each troop who then read the mileometers and sent them back to me. Now if at some stage the speedometers had been replaced it seemed that no one noted this, so the readings were nothing like the readings for the previous month. It took me some time to get the troops to notice this problem.

It was not long before the Regiment went on an exercise to exercise the tank crews. The tanks had to be moved to an infamous training area called Saltau, infamous due to the fact that the soil in this area was black and in the summer it was black dust we had to endure and in the winter it was black mud.

The troop had to bring with them the stores, which were caged in the back of three ton trucks specially adapted for this purpose. I was selected to drive one of these together with the large accommodation trailer behind. When we reached the first location we had to camouflage the vehicles and set up to be able to issue any spare item of stores continuously.

A funny incident occurred during my first such exercise. It happened during the drive down to Sotau. I had travelled some miles to the autobahn and turned onto the autobahn where I had to travel further and then get onto another autobahn. As I approached the turn I put on my indicator. This was situated on the dashboard in the form of a switch which you switched to right or left and then when the turn had been completed you then switched it back to the central position.

I turned onto the autobahn and reached over to return the indicator to the central position and in doing so the switch just simply fell to pieces. Panic ensued for now I could not get the indicator off without stopping and as you were not allowed to stop in the middle of an Army convoy I was up the proverbial creek without an indicator, so to speak.

CoH Eddie Shotton who was my co-driver managed to lean out of his window unscrew the indicator glass and remove the bulb, but my side was still flashing and this it did until we eventually got off the autobahn and I could stop and do some running repairs. It took me some time to live this down with the troop for I was christened

LG Tech Troop at 'Communion' Soltau 1974
Capt (Rev) Greaves SQMC(E) (Rev) Johnson LCOH Shortman LCOH Harrison COH Edge

'Winker' Jack by the SQMC Don Johnson and that nickname has stuck even to this day.

It was about this time that my wife informed that I was to be a father for the fourth time. I was overjoyed and we began planning ahead as the Regiment was due for a tour in Northern Ireland the next year so we made a decision that Mary would go home to 'Mum' during the time I was in NI, just in case anything happened to me.

The year ended and I was sent on a Technical Storeman's Course at BOD (Brigade Ordnance Depot) Veirsen Germany and passing this gave me more scope in the role I had in the stores.

At the end of 1971 and the beginning of 1972 the Regiment began training as foot soldiers for the tour of NI. This meant forming Companies of soldiers and the forming of a Tac HQ (Tactical Headquarters) to which I was posted as a Signaller in the Operations room. I also had to undergo the rigorous training to get fit and get used to the SLR Rifle we were equipped with.

Regarding the SLR Rifle, I had been involved with the transportation of some 500 rifles from Command Ordnance Depot, Donnington before the Regiment's move to Germany, as it was known then of this posting. The transportation of such weaponry was, to say the least, dangerous. The transport of three trucks carrying all the rifles and accessories had to move from Donnington in Shropshire to Windsor non-stop with an armed escort.

The training for NI was now in full swing. We were taught Judo and rifle drill and also trained in the Sennelager training area. The Regiment had taken over a Camp from the Bundeswehr (German Army) which was called Staumuhle in a specially constructed 'City' constructed of corrugated sheets. This was to ensure we knew what to do when on foot patrols in the area of Belfast we were to go to.

I was now getting the hang of the Ops room organisation. We had three Royal Signals chaps with us commanded by a Lieutenant Knock. We were to do nine hour shifts with two fully trained signallers on duty, one on the radio sets and one to look after the

The Life Guards Tech Troop Soltau circa 1974
COH Edge Tpr Shaw and Smith COH Bourne Capt Greaves Tpr unknown
LCOH Shortman SQMC(E) Johnson LCOH Harrison

teleprinter which we also had to be trained to operate.

It was during this training that one day Lieutenant Knock came into the mock Ops Room carrying a bottle of champagne, which he plonked down on the table in front of me and said casually that I owed everyone a drink from this bottle. For once lost for words I eventually managed to ask what the hell was going on and he said that I would have to buy these drinks for was I not improperly dressed.

I at once started to look myself over, which set everyone off laughing. "No, on your arm Lance Corporal," eventually gasped Lieutenant Knock. I suddenly realised that he was referring to promotion. I was overjoyed as this meant a leap in pay as well as Sergeants' Mess status.

I will explain, I believe that the Life Guards are the only Regiment to have lance corporals in their Sergeants' Mess hence it was called WOs and NCOs Mess. Unfortunately because of space in the barracks it was impossible to have one mess, so the lance corporals had a small mess below the proper mess. As was the tradition we all trooped off to the said mess where I had to buy the drinks all round. Later on, much the worse for wear, I dragged myself home, much to the disgust of my wife until she learned of my promotion.

The time came for Mary to leave for UK in readiness for our fourth child and to arrange schooling for the two girls (Andrew was not yet school age). It was with great emotion that I said goodbye to them at Gütersloh airport, at least my wife would have her parents' support whilst I was away.

The Regiment left for NI at the end of July 1972 and was split into HQ Squadron, Admin Squadron, two Rifle Squadrons and a 6 Troop (Assault Troop). RHQ would be housed in a police station (Mount Pottinger), Admin was to be housed in two old ships called the *Maidstone* and *Hartland Point*. The Rifle Squadrons were to be housed in various other parts of Belfast. The whole Regiment was made up of various other Regiments who came under our Colonel's Command and was called The Life Guards' Group.

I soon got into the swing of routine that we had trained for. Most of my time was taken up with duty in the Operations' room monitoring the radio nets. My off duty periods were mostly spent trying to get some sleep. This was not made easy as we were cramped for room and if I remember correctly there were about ten of us in one small room.

The tedium was relieved from time to time by what we called an SDS run. This consisted of two of us and a driver (Landrover) plying from Rifle Squadrons to the Admin Squadron with signal messages etc. There were four of us on a regular basis, myself, Gordie Dickson, Corporal Donnan and Trooper Burk, the driver.

These runs tended to be done at a great speed with two of us standing on the rear tail board to give cover. This was 'hairy' to say the least especially with Trooper Burk's driving and Corporal Donnan's constant demands to fire his 'rubber bullets' at everything that moved.

On one such run with myself and Gordie, we were stopped by a very agitated Irishman. I asked him what was the trouble. "There is a strange car parked outside my house and there are some wires hanging from the boot." "Have you touched it?" I asked. "No, but my son has cut the wires," he replied with some pride. "Where is this car," I asked with some trepidation, hoping it was somewhere in the Irish sea, just for safety's sake you understand.

"It's here," he said pointing to the car we were standing next to. To say that both Gordie and I panicked would be a slight untruth, but we did tell the Irish gentlemen to get inside his house. We did this as we reversed rather hurriedly the way we had come and at the same time reporting this incident over the radio. We found out later that it was a false alarm, but in those days it could easily have been the real thing.

We did get on the 'streets' from time to time mostly giving escort to intelligence searches. These were not without some funny incidents. The most vivid to me was the time when I was guarding our Regimental carpenter who had been called to re-hang a front door of a local Irish family who had been 'searched' that morning and the door had been smashed in and as nothing had been found we had to repair the door.

I was alert watching for 'snipers' when a youth approached me. He was about fifteen as I recall and when he asked me if he could see my rifle I became rather more alert. However I managed to persuade him that it was not a good idea to ask me that. He seemed to lose interest, but then asked me what religion I was.

I thought about this and as I was rather 'jarred off' with this particular youth I answered "I am agnostic". I could tell he did not know what this meant and went away with a strange look on his face. I thought maybe I could use this ploy again if I came across another obnoxious youth again.

Our 6 Troop was kept very busy during those first few weeks in Belfast dealing with one riot after another. There was a local works that employed only one faction of local Irishmen and women and they had to walk through the other faction housing estate on their way to and from work. These people had to be escorted down these streets, a dangerous and un-appealing job.

In the middle of August I was informed by our Operation Officer Major Willy Lloyd that I had become a father again. I rang home immediately to discover that Mary had given birth to a daughter and that we were to call her Amanda. I was granted some leave which we called R & R (Rest and Recuperation). I managed to get four days and almost immediately got on a flight from Aldergrove Belfast to Speke Airport in Liverpool, being the nearest to where my wife was living.

I spent a very happy three days with my family as it was August Bank Holiday weekend. However it came all too soon to say goodbye again. I had to get a taxi to the nearest railway station which would get me to Crewe. When I reached Crewe I discovered to my horror that the next train to Liverpool would not get me there in reasonable time to get me to the airport for my flight and it would be cutting it very fine indeed.

I had no option but to catch the train. I sat on the edge of my seat all the journey hoping that the train would not be late. It arrived on time and I shot out of the station to find a taxi. I explained to the taxi driver my predicament and he said he would try and get me there on time. We shot off a great speed, well at least as fast as he could go being that he had a clapped out old Hackney cab which tended to shake uncontrollably anywhere over the speed of 30m.p.h.

Whilst heading down a dual carriageway doing about sixty we were overtaken by a police car who promptly pulled us over. I started to panic at this stage, but when I showed the policeman my ID card and explained I had to be on this flight, all was saved.

The policeman said that I could travel with them and after an assurance that the good taxi driver would not be fined, I offered to pay the taxi, but he refused. The police car set off at incredible speed and he radioed ahead for the flight to be held for me. We arrived at the airport with only minutes to spare and after thanking the police I got aboard. I shall always remember those policemen and for that matter the taxi driver and his cab.

The days drew on into weeks and I managed to get a day R & R with Gordie Dickson. A Navy Mine Sweeper had offered to take a

Lcpl Leach myself Saltau training area Germany 1974

couple of the lads on a day trip across to the Isle of Man. So Gordie and I managed to get 'invited'. We got aboard in the early morning and got under way, but as we got further into the Irish Sea the Captain said that it was too rough to go all the way across.

So instead we were given a tour of the ship and it was explained to us how the mines were 'swept' and we had a go at steering the ship. We had our lunch in their ORs mess which we found consisted of mainly sandwiches and beer with the emphasis on the beer, there seemed to be an unending supply of it. So Gordie and I got into the spirit of the mess so to speak so it was with some trouble that we clambered off the ship after we had returned.

The transport was waiting for us and by the time we had got back to Mountpottinger it was getting extremely late. We entered the station and made our way to the Operations' room where we had to book in. We were both the worse for wear and an argument ensued outside the OPs room as to who would enter and book us in.

Gordie insisted that as I was senior to him it was my duty. I pointed out to him that as he was my junior he should obey my order. We decided to compromise. We should both go in together. This, as it turned out, was a mistake. We had forgotten in our present state that there was a very deep step down into the OPs room. We opened the door and stepped in, overbalanced and crashed to the floor.

This would have been OK had not the CO been sitting in his accustomed chair near to the door. We landed in a heap at his feet, whereupon he looked down at us and said rather sarcastically, "I know that I am your Commanding Officer but there is no need to grovel at my feet, you may stand up gentlemen and book in, and consider that you will do two extra Sanger duties in the near future." (Sanger being to look out posts around the station) we retreated rather shamefacedly.

This officer did have a sense of humour. I was on duty in the Telex room, Gordie was in the OPs room, when the intercom buzzed. Thinking it was Gordie wanting more tea, I answered, "Mount Pottinger Asylum, duty idiot speaking." There was a long pause, then a cultured voice replied, "Probably you are Lance Corporal, but I would like a cup of tea." It was the CO! I was very careful after that when answering the intercom.

For obvious reasons I cannot dwell too much on this tour except to say that the Regiment did very well for its first time as an Infantry Regiment although there was one sad note as LCoH Len Durber was seriously injured and remained in a coma until February 1973 when he sadly died. This was the only serious injury sustained by The Life Guards' Group. When we had returned to Detmold a Special Order of the day was issued to all ranks outlining the Regiment's achievements during its tour.

CHAPTER TEN.

DEMOLD, CANADA AND UK

The Regiment was now into November and getting ready to hand over to 42 Squadron Royal Engineers and flew back to BAOR on 30 November. We had all received a month's leave and I had organised that I flew back to UK a few days after arriving in BAOR. I had also organised flights back for all my family.

I flew over on 2 December and was once again reunited with my family. The new baby was growing so fast that I hardly recognised her from the tiny thing I had seen in August. Mary and I proceeded to do the rounds of the family and I hired a car and we did a tour of Wales.

During this happy time we had the Christening of our latest daughter and I asked a couple of the lads up as godfathers. Geff Randle a trumpeter we had befriended acted as godfather and another trumpeter came up to join in the celebrations. Bob Owen in fact came from West Felton near Oswestry and is now the Band Master of the Blues and Royal Band with the rank of major.

There was a sad time during this leave. My father-in-law became very ill and had to go into hospital. He had silicosis of the lungs. This was not surprising as he had worked down the local pit for over forty years. However his health improved before we left to go back to Germany.

The time came to leave and we said goodbye to Mary's family who had been so good and understanding during the last few months. I said goodbye to my father-in-law with whom I had had a few beers during my leave, and we set off for RAF Hendon where we would stay overnight and fly out the next day. The flight was uneventful and we arrived back in our quarter in the late afternoon.

We had planned to have a quiet weekend after the hectic last few weeks, but it was not to be.

I was awakened very early on the Sunday morning by the Regiment's duty driver, who said that the Orderly Corporal Major wanted me in to the barracks to do a duty. As I was not due back until the following day, I did not take kindly to this message, but as this seemed to be a direct order I very reluctantly dressed in civilian clothes and went into barracks.

Upon arriving at the Guard room the duty Corporal Major greeted me and told me not to fly off the handle, it was the only way he could get me into barracks. He then informed me the very sad news that my father-in-law had died the previous evening. He told me breaking the news to my wife would be better done by me and not the duty officer.

The news of course stunned me as I had a great regard for Mary's father. I now had the terrible task of telling Mary and the children. When I got back home Mary at once knew there was something wrong. She was distraught so I went next door and asked a very good neighbour to come and sit with her whilst I went back to barracks and tried to organise a flight of some description.

I could not get everything organised that day so I went back to normal duties on the Monday. Major Greeves was most helpful and managed to organise a trip home with the Regimental mini bus as I was not entitled at that time to any free flights home. This did not cost too much as the cost was subsidised by the Regimental PRI fund.

Because of the two elder girls' schooling we left them to be looked after by our neighbour and we set off together with the two smaller children. The journey was long and tedious and we arrived home the day before the funeral and set off back the day after, arriving back in Detmold on the following Friday. To say the least, a week I would not wish to live through again.

The new year began with the usual diary dates as to when the Regiment would be going on various exercises and Tank training in Soltah etc. I was told that I would be going on a B1 Clerk's course later on in the year. I would be locally in Veirsen where I had taken my Tech Storeman's course. I duly went on this course and passed with a good pass mark.

The Regiment had its yearly inspection by the Divisional Commander. This Commander on the actual day would order each Squadron to complete a task. e.g. one Squadron would lay out its kit by their tanks, another would have its accommodation block ready for inspection etc. The recce part of one Squadron was sent with full kit to Denmark to retrieve a certain object from a certain place and return within a specific period of time.

My Squadron had to parade on the square if I remember right. 'Jumbo' Greaves was asked quite casually by the Commander to produce a Regimental Band for this parade. How he managed this I will never know, but he did.

It was about this time that we had persuaded Mary's mother to come over to Germany and spend some time with the family. We chose to get her on a coach ride from Dover by a coach run by a Regiment in Hobart Barracks, the other barracks in the town. She chose to travel with a friend's daughter Jane, who was also a friend of my two elder daughters.

She arrived whilst I was still on my course, so when I got back we took her for a night out in my mess. This was on a Saturday night and we had a good time. The following Monday morning I had to go in front of my CO for a course report. The CO in question was Lieutenant Colonel Bradish-Ellames (he of the Mount Pottinger Asylum!). I was marched into his office and stood to attention whilst he read my course report and my personal file.

After a while he congratulated me on my course report and asked my why I had enlisted in the RA I told him that was the only way I could find to finally get into the Life Guards. He thought about this for a moment and then said, "Well Lance Corporal Shortman I really do believe in loyalty in a person and as I see that you have been loyal to your Regiment, perhaps you would like to march out promoted to LCoH."

I saluted in a daze and was marched out by RCM 'Lofty' Young, who was as much bemused by this event as I was. "I do not know how this happened LCoH, but you had better get yourself over to

Headquarters Squadron October 1978 GOC's annual inspection
I am fourth from right front rank

the mess and certainly buy me a very stiff drink." It took me a long while to convince Mary that I had once again been promoted.

Even more to explain to Mary's mother why we were drinking in a different mess the following Saturday.

It was about this time that the mess was organising a mess football team to challenge other Sergeants' Messes in the surrounding area. As I was then and always have been a keen supporter of football, I put my name down for this activity. The matches were to be held on a Sunday on a home and away basis. My mess would entertain another mess, play the game and have a lunch in the mess afterwards.

This event went on for a considerable time and the amount of cars leaving barracks on a Sunday became more as the weeks went by, more with supporters than footballers. After all we all had a good time whether we lost or won.

There had been changes in my troop, with 'Kiwi' Howells leaving and SQMC Cornish taking his place, Bill Bourne getting his CoH and Charlie Harrison getting promoted to LCoH. The usual round of exercises to Saltau. Life with the Regiment settled down again.

Things began to change for my family and I that year. I had applied for a larger MQ now that our fourth child had appeared and was granted one which turned out to be a three bedroom house the other side of town and nearer the barracks. It was also the time that I bought my first car as I now enjoyed a better life style due to my promotion and the higher rate of pay that went with it.

I had bought a large Peugeot Estate car which I could comfortably fit my family into. I also invested in a tent and all the camping gear as my family had expressed an interest in camping for some time. A rather embarrassing incident took place just after I had bought the car.

The Regiment was due to go to Soltau for training and one of the jobs of our QM(E) 'Jumbo' Greaves was to ensure that all out Chieftain tanks were loaded onto the train properly. The tanks always had to go to the training area either by train or by tank transporters, as they were not allowed on the roads for obvious reasons.

Me 'Dry' Skiing Scotland 1977

Me Mary Irene and Sgt Randy Scott USA 1977 WO's Mess

'Jumbo' had asked me to run him down to the railway station in my new car (I secretly thought that he only wanted to see what it was like). I agreed and we climbed into the 'new' car but as I selected first gear to my intense horror the gear stick snapped and I was left holding just the top half of said gear stick. I was never more embarrassed than at that moment. The car was off the road for some time until the local garage could get a spare gear stick.

Towards the end of 1973 the Regiment was told that it had to go once again to NI (in those days the turn around of Regiments for this posting was very quick). To my relief I was told that I would be remaining in Germany with the rear party.

The Regimental training began in the new year. I would then be doing a Duty Clerk's role whilst the Regiment was away. This was a whole weekend duty commencing at 4.30 p.m. Friday until 8 o'clock the following Monday. There was a bed and eating utensils. The duty cook had to bring over my meals. This duty turned out to be on the whole a very lonesome and boring duty.

Another 'duty' I had to perform was that of a 'Regimental Father' to a number of wives of our lads that were in NI. My duty towards them was that I went to their quarters and asked them if they needed anything e.g. repairs to their quarters, financial help etc. One lady, the wife of Lance Corporal Balnaves, called Hilary was new to the Army life and was at that time expecting her first child.

So my wife seemed to take her under her wing and we became very friendly and with her husband Dale. I liked to joke with her saying as the child was due in May of that year she must "hold on" until the 23rd, as it was my birthday. This she promised to do and low and behold she did and the child was born on my birthday. Ever since then I have never failed to send a birthday card to that child.

About half way through the Regiment's tour of NI I was on one of my weekend duties when two incidents took place which taxed my clerical knowledge. A certain REME soldier attached to the Regiment in NI had flown home to Scotland to be with his wife and her parents.

London Underground Flood Centre 1977 during the firemen's strike. I am standing far right.

Remembrance Sunday Combermere Barracks 1977

He had flown back to NI and his wife's parents and taken his wife to the airport to return to Germany. On the way back they had crashed and were killed. I had to get him back from NI to Germany and organise a flight back from Germany to Scotland. Whilst I was getting around this problem another soldier attached to the Regiment in NI had a death in his family and I had to organise this too. You could bet that I did not have a boring weekend.

Once again the Regiment returned and life settled down to the routine. Once again we were on exercise at the dreaded Saltau. It was at the time getting cold on this exercise so the QM (E) produced a bottle of Cherry Brandy for the troop (just a nip to keep the cold out you understand, he said).

This became a ritual each morning for each one in the troop to have a nip. So it was decided by someone, who shall remain nameless, that one should have 'holy communion'. 'Jumbo' Greaves dressed in an old bed sheet and SQMC Don Johnson similarly attired acted as the 'Clergy' and myself, Charlie Harrison and CoH Reg Edge solemnly took our 'wine'. It was rumoured that some other soldiers of the Regiment when hearing of this decided that they also would like early morning 'wine', but this was not proved.

As the Regiment entered 1975 the activity increased to fever pitch as this was the year that we were to be going back to our home base in Windsor and the Regiment had also to gear up for a move to Suffield, Canada for some training. Suffield was a huge training area in Alberta near to a large town called Medicine Hat.

The Regiment flew from Gütersloh first to Iceland where we stopped a couple of hours and then flew onto Calgary. This was a long journey and all of us were 'jet lagged' when we arrived. We also had some 150 miles to travel from Calgary to our barracks. When we arrived and started getting ready for our first exercise the weather took a turn for the very worse.

Some four foot of snow fell on the training area making it completely unfit to do any training at all. The Commanding Officer decided that some R & R was to take place. I cannot remember how I and seven other soldiers were chosen to spend some time on a Canadian ranch near a place called Okatoks. However that is where I landed up just a few days after arriving in Canada.

I had become very good friends with Doug Skelly who worked as a LCoH Mess Steward in the Officers' Mess and as luck would have it we were together on this ranch. The ranch was owned by a gentleman by the name of Edward McNally and the ranch bred Aberdeen Angus bulls. We were made extremely welcome and were shown to a 'summer house' where we were told that all the facilities including food were available to us as long as we were there.

Our host laid on the next day a variety of ·22 rifles for us to shoot gophers, which were a burrowing animal resembling our grey squirrel. These animals were extremely bad pests as they burrowed under the crops eating the shoots causing great damage. We had a great time trying to shoot them. We also had access to the cow ponies that were stabled there.

These were, at first, difficult to ride as they were trained to different commands than our horses, but we managed and had a good time on them. Our host also asked us if we could plant some trees on the edge of one of his fields. These would act as a wind break to stop the wind erosions of the soil. We of course agreed and duly planted them. Our host I believe named that line of trees 'Life Guard Avenue' although I have not been back to see.

Our ranching life came to an end after some ten days as the weather had cleared and we all returned to Suffield Barracks, but not before our host had taken all of us together with his family for a night out at the local bar. Sufficient to say a good time was had by one and all, at least I think it was, as I only have a hazy recollection of the proceedings.

Doug Skelly and I had become very firm friends and spent most of our free time together. This friendship remained for a very long time until sadly he died in 1994. Mary and I still keep close contact with his widow Sonia and his children. Doug and I had made friends with a Canadian family living in Medicine Hat, if I recall right they were Alva and Roger, I cannot remember their surname.

Alva was supposedly directly descended from Sitting Bull the great Sioux chieftain, although this was never proved.

It was one Saturday night in a local pub in Medicine Hat that a funny incident took place, although it could have turned out nasty. We had serving with us one Trooper Brown, known as 'Twitcher', this was because he had a slight affliction where he had some sort of muscle twitch. As I said we were sitting in this bar, about six of us, and sitting directly behind 'Twitcher' was a Canadian couple.

All of a sudden 'Twitcher' decided that he would have one of his 'twitches' whilst just about to take swig at his glass. The result was almost catastrophic. The said beverage shot out of the glass and deposited itself all down the lady's dress. She shot to her feet, reasonably so I thought given the circumstances, and promptly knocked over the table depositing their drinks over her husband.

It took us the rest of the evening to persuade the couple, especially the husband, who stood about six foot nine, that the aforesaid 'Twitcher' did not mean to soak his wife. It also cost us a considerable amount of money buying drinks and offering to pay for the cleaning of the said clothes. We succeeded in the end, all of us getting quite drunk.

All too soon we had to say goodbye to our Canadian friends and we flew back to Germany on my birthday. When we arrived back we had no respite as we all had to get ready to hand over and go back to UK. The main party would be going back in the October and the advanced party a few weeks before this to take over the barracks at Windsor and to take over all the married quarters.

I found out that I had been allocated a quarter in Cavalry Crescent which was next to the barracks and that it was two old quarters knocked into one so that I could have four bedrooms, but more of that later.

The time came to hand over my MQ, Mary was to fly with the children and I was to drive back with some of our possessions. I handed over the MQ successfully and set off for Zeebruge together with my wife's houseplants, radio, mops, buckets etc. I had two passengers, Lance Corporal John O'Connell and a trooper whose name I cannot recall. John was a member of the Tech Troop whom

I had made friends with.

We set off making our way down the autobahn to catch the midnight ferry arriving in Dover the next morning. I had some difficulty in getting through Customs, not because of booze or cigarettes, but because the chassis number and engine number on my car appeared to be the same. After some consultation with customs officials we were allowed to go on to Windsor.

We arrived sometime in the afternoon and I deposited my passengers at the barracks and went around to Cavalry Crescent to find my MQ. The MQ consisted of two MQs knocked into one with two of everything. My daughters were quite excited at having two bathrooms and two kitchens. We unpacked and as we were still waiting for our MFO to arrive made the best we could with what we had got.

I was on leave for a couple of weeks so after settling the three children into their school (Amanda was still only three) we settled down to life once again in Windsor. Upon return to duty Captain Graves informed me that I would in fact be looking after a store on my own. The Tech had taken over an Arctic clothing store from the Blues and Royals, as one of the Squadrons would be on an Arctic training, this turned out to be C Squadron.

The store was equipped with everything that would be necessary for the Squadron to operate in arctic conditions from parkas to tents and thermal clothing. Because it was such a large store I had help with Trooper Brown who had not long joined the troop and who had passed his Tech courses. He was to be promoted to Lance Corporal because of the responsibility of the amount of stores we had to account for.

The Christmas period came and went with all the usual parties etc., including the Regimental WOs and NCOs mess brick hanging. Let me explain as best I can for I do not know of the exact history of this tradition. The tradition has apparently been handed down for some considerable time; (the hundredth brick hanging was in 1989, 100 'Brick Hanging' medals were struck and as I was present at this event I managed to obtain one by payment).

On the day the serving members of the Regiment assemble in the mess in the lounge bar and are issued with broom handles. They then march into the other bar singing the regimental hymn "Lloyd George knew my father, my father knew Lloyd George" and beating the handle on the floor. Non serving members greet them and the past serving RCM would then hang the brick on a hook above the bar and christen it with whisky. The 'Brick' is of small dimensions and is banded by silver bands. After this ceremony we all usually get rather drunk.

As Christmas came nearer I was asked by the RCM, who by this time was RCM Les Lumb, if I would do Squadron Orderly Corporal for Christmas day and Boxing day as I lived near the barracks and I was not going away. I was assured I would get days off in lieu so I agreed. The two days passed peacefully with no alarms.

1976 started off well with C Squadron going off to Norway for their first Arctic training. It was a great deal of work issuing out all the necessary equipment to each individual, in fact all the troop were involved. Things calmed down after this until the Squadron returned and all the equipment had to be taken back into store and inspected for defects etc.

Then came the long period of 'writing off' equipment that could not be repaired and of course demanding replacement items to bring the store up to the amount of stock we were entitled to. After this daily routine began to get back to normal and I managed to get some more leave.

As the year went on it became increasingly difficult to afford to run my rather large car due to the cost of petrol in the UK (we had all been used to cheap fuel in Germany) so I sold it and bought a smaller car.

The year went on with the usual training and parades. One Squadron went off to the USA to take over a tank unit there and their Squadron came over to see how we ran our Regiment. We had many a good night in the mess with these American soldiers. We were all amused to see and hear them when they went on training runs. They carried their Squadron or unit flag and sang all the way.

We met a Sergeant Randy Smock who turned out to be a very

accomplished singer and guitar player. My daughter Irene I believe had some sort of young lady's crush on him, but nothing came of it.

During this year Doug Skelly finished his time and went off into civvy street, going to live in Peterborough with his family. This was a sad time as my family and his had formed a close friendship. However I was to meet him again when I was demobbed.

The year came and went very quickly with the Squadron returning from the USA and the Regiment saying farewell to the Americans with a final American type barbecue in the mess. I was then asked by the RCM to be part of a committee to organise a Christmas mess raffle. The day arrived and it all went off very well I thought. I was surprised when I received a letter from the RCM thanking me for the way I had organised the event, all the committee got the same letter I believe. 1977 dawned and in February George Dugdale who was still in the orderly room asked if I would like to go on a 'Battle field tour' of the battle fields of the Second World War, specifically the Battle of the Ardennes known as the Battle of the 'Bulge'. I said I would love to go and obtained permission from Captain Greaves to be allowed away from my duties for the period. He agreed.

However Mary did not agree believing this to be a somewhat boozy affair. However together with George's wife Janet persuaded that it would not be so, she was mollified by the suggestion that she and Janet visited the Dutch bulb fields whilst George and I were away. She agreed so I had to pay for the trip.

George and I duly departed for Belgium and ended up in mess accommodation in a Belgium Artillery Barracks in Bastion. This is where most of the battle was fought in and around this town. We set off each day with different guides who turned out to be senior ranks in the armies. There was a colonel from an American unit, a major from the English unit and a very senior officer from a German unit.

On one of the days we were taken through a wood where the English major had taken his unit the evening before attacking the Germans in a village. They had dug in and awaited the orders to attack. The major showed us where they had dug their trenches, which were still there albeit nearly filled in. He pointed out where he thought his trench was and upon kicking some of the dirt away came across an old army mess tin, very rusty. Upon closer inspection he discovered that his name was on the tin, what a discovery.

The last day we did a tour of the battlefield of the Battle of Waterloo and we were guided through the events of that day. It was very eerie to think that both the Regiments in which I had served fought and died here. My Commanding Officer of my Cyprus days would have liked to be there I am sure, as his direct descendant, the Duke of Wellington commanded the British forces on that day.

We had had a very interesting time on that tour and I enjoyed it very much. Once again C Squadron were off to Norway and the round of issuing kit and receiving it back came around, we were getting very proficient at this procedure by this time.

I was also off on my travels again, this time skiing in Scotland where the Brigade had a ski lodge near a place called Blairgowery near Perth. I volunteered to try out this skiing lark, much to the consternation of my wife.

I set out with Toby Carrington; he was a clerk in the Regimental orderly room, by train. This turned out to be a long and tedious journey. When we eventually arrived at this ski lodge we were housed with about a dozen other members of the Brigade of Guards.

We were all issued with warm clothing and the necessary ski equipment and the next day set off for the 'learner' slopes. We all had a few falls, but I enjoyed this new 'sport'. We all became fairly proficient, but only on the very shallow slopes.

During this time we were all asked if we would like to go on a grouse shoot as the 'Glorious Twelfth' would soon be upon us. Most of us volunteered except me. I knew what this would entail, it would mean 'beating' through the heather getting very dirty and tired. I opted to go trout fishing in the local river.

We all had a day doing 'grass skiing'. This was done with a special type of roller skis down sloping fields next to the ski lodge. It rained that day and we all got extremely wet and muddy. The day was rounded off with a good booze up.

I did travel up again to the lodge later on. I remember travelling up by Landrover stopping overnight at the Sergeants' Mess in Catterick Camp. Incidentally the Garrison Sergeant Major was an old 'Blue' WO2 'Ginger' Storey whom I served with in my National Service days in Cyprus.

I had had a problem with a nasty sore on my right shin, which would not heal, and the Regimental Medical Officer, Surgeon Major Stewart, decided that the cause of this was poor circulation stemming from a varicose vein. So he booked me into the Cambridge Military Hospital in Aldershot to have the offending vein removed.

I duly arrived at the hospital and I had to wait a couple of days for the operation. When the day dawned I was awakened by a fearfully starched captain in the QARANC (Queen Alexandra's Royal Army Nursing Corps) and she ordered me to have a bath and then she would have a nurse shave the necessary parts of my leg.

When this nurse appeared she turned out to be a trainee nurse and to say the least a little shy of shaving the necessary parts. She however managed the bottom half of my leg, but when she got to the top I could see that her hand was not as steady as I would like it to be considering where the said razor would be shaving. I thought that I should better take charge so I finished off the shaving much to the relief of the young nurse.

The operation went well and I remained in hospital for a few more days and then returned back to Windsor and was placed on sick leave for two weeks. The leg was bandaged from toe to crutch and had to be changed daily and I could not get it wet so bathing was a big problem, however I managed.

As the year progressed the fire brigade began its threatened strike so the Regiment was called into action to crew the Army's fire fighting vehicles widely known as 'Green Goddesses'. Because of my clerking skills I was selected with others in the Regiment to work alongside the fire service white-collar workers to man the operations room in the Flood Centre in London which was underground.

In this capacity I was involved with sending the fire engines to various fires all over London. This was a totally enthralling job and I will always remember those two weeks or so and wonder in awe at the dedication of the fire service.

Back in Windsor the celebrations of the Queen's Silver Jubilee were in full swing with children's parties, mess parties etc., culminating in the bonfire and fireworks in Windsor Great Park attended by Her Majesty. 1977 was coming to an end and I had made the decision to finish my army career the next year so Mary and I started to get our things together and the orderly room organised a demob course for me in Aldershot. Meanwhile the usual Christmas festivities took place, the 'Brick Hanging' and the mess raffle.

1978 dawned and I was asked by the Chief Clerk if I would like to go and run a Regimental souvenir stall at Whitehall selling souvenirs to the public. The stall was situated in Horse Guards where the Queen's Life Guards paraded. I said I would and this proved another insight into diversity of the British soldier. I had never sold anything in my life, but I managed to sell quite a lot of the goods on offer over the two weeks I was there.

May came around and I set off on my demob course which was for a month and it was a bricklaying course. I passed as I had done three years as an apprentice before my National Service.

After this I took some leave and went up to Peterborough to see Doug Skelly and his family and to seek employment there. I managed not only to find employment, but also to acquire a house. The local council said that a house would be available when I was finally demobbed and the local private school that had a permanent work force assured me the job was open for me.

This issue now settled together with the children's schooling (my elder daughters had left school by this time) I settled down to organising our last move etc. It was at this time that I was ordered to see the Commanding Officer who at this time was Lieutenant Colonel Hartigan. The Colonel informed me that I would be allowed to go on leave from August until my demob in December, but as there was an annual Brigade inspection of the Regiment I would be required to be present on that parade.

I enjoyed some weeks of freedom and various parties in the mess so when the day came along for the Regimental parade I duly cleaned my kit, pinned on my medals for the last time and went on parade.

The inspecting officer was Brigadier Eyres, who was my Squadron Leader in Germany when I was in the 'Blues'. When he inspected me he remembered me, and asked how my family and I were. The parade went off okay and I returned to my MQ.

However the Chief Clerk sent for me for he had been asked by the Brigadier why I had not been awarded the Long Service and Good Conduct medal. I said I did not know why so there was a bit of a flap on until they found out that I had not gone quite the eighteen years from my offence at Knightsbridge, so I was not entitled to the medal. You can't win them all.

The sad day in December came all too quickly and I said goodbye to all my friends and comrades. Mary and the family had already moved up to Peterborough so all that remained for me to do was to get my papers. In retrospect I made a wrong decision in coming out when I did and I have kicked myself many times over for making that decision.

I enjoyed all my service, and I would not change any of it. I made a lot of friends and enjoyed their comradeship, their sense of humour, but most of all their friendship. I have kept in touch with a lot of these and still enjoy their company when we meet. I now go on to enjoy another challenge in my life.

MEMOIRS OF A SOLDIER IN THE HOUSEHOLD CAVALRY